How to Speak Money

How to Speak Money

THE LANGUAGE AND KNOWLEDGE
YOU NEED NOW

Ali Velshi and Christine Romans

WILEY

John Wiley & Sons, Inc.

Published by John Wiley & Sons, Inc., Hoboken, New Jersey.
Published simultaneously in Canada.

For general information on our other products and services or for technical support, please contact our Customer Care Department within the United States at (800) 762-2974, outside the United States at (317) 572-3993 or fax (317) 572-4002.

Wiley also publishes its books in a variety of electronic formats. Some content that appears in print may not be available in electronic books. For more information about Wiley products, visit our web site at www.wiley.com.

Library of Congress Cataloging-in-Publication Data:'
Velshi, Ali.
   How to speak money : the language and knowledge you need now / Ali Velshi and Christine Romans.
     p. cm.
   Includes bibliographical references and index.
   ISBN 978-1-118-11495-7 (cloth); ISBN 978-1-118-19337-2 (ebk);
ISBN 978-1-118-19339-6 (ebk); ISBN 978-1-118-19338-9 (ebk)
     1. Finance, Personal. 2. Money. I. Romans, Christine, 1971- II. Title.
HG179.V45 2012
332.024—dc23

                                 2011033518

Printed in the United States of America
10 9 8 7 6 5 4 3 2 1

To Ed and Lori.

Contents

Acknowledgments

Special thanks to Tom Wynbrandt. Without his collaboration, this book would not have happened. Also to our morning business producer Katy Byron, the excellent staffs of CNN's *Your Bottom Line, Your Money,* and *American Morning,* and a special mention to our intelligent, enlightened, and visionary bosses and executive producers (see Chapter 5: How to Speak Jobs) at CNN for giving us the platform on which to Speak Money. Thanks to CNN president Ken Jautz who, 10 years ago, put us together on the anchor desk and sparked a collaboration that led to this book. You have good taste.

The folks at CNNMoney.com inspire and educate us every day. And of course our respective spouses speak money better than we do and have taught us that money is secondary to that other valuable language—compromise.

Introduction

Why We've Written This Book

Welcome to *How to Speak Money*.

Allow us to introduce ourselves. Christine and Ali are colleagues at CNN; both business reporters and anchors. Like many co-workers, we spend more time at work with each other than we do with our spouses. We've also grown to be friends and confidants—partners in financial (reporting) crime—over the past 10 years. I'm not sure looking back to when we met at work 10 years ago that we would have thought we'd be this tight a decade later. Back then, our differences—in our backgrounds and in our approaches to money—were greater than our similarities. Or at least that's what we thought.

The biggest thing we had going for our relationship over the years is that we spoke the same language. We're not talking about English. We were both fluent in the language of money. We understood terms like "12-month trailing revenue" and "slow stochastics" and we relished the latest news about the 200-day moving average. Business geeks, indeed. Truly, there wasn't a ton we had in common other than that we understood very clearly what the other said when we spoke in story meetings and on TV. (We share a love of high-caloric food; but that's for another book.)

Over the years, by force and by choice, we ended up working very closely together; more so than we did with other co-workers. Our perspectives were different, but complimentary. We'd fill in for each other when one of us was sick, we'd help each other solve problems. Once in a while, we'd grab lunch or an after-work drink.

Like co-workers, or any pair, who spend a lot of time together, we fought. The fight we remember most clearly was years ago when Christine seemed overly excited about the danger of the U.S. credit rating being downgraded. Ali thought it was unimportant. The fight may seem unimportant to you, but back when it was happening, we were pretty passionate about our positions on it. Turns out that Christine was right to be as concerned as she was. Ultimately, years later, the U.S. credit rating was downgraded. Christine remains kind enough not to remind Ali about that fight. Many of our fights turn out that way. Many of yours probably do, too.

And like many good pairs—be they spouses, business partners, roommates, siblings, parents/kids—we learned from each other and about each other, we grew, and we grew to better understand and appreciate each other. And while we always spoke each other's language, now we can even write and speak like the other. Can you guess which one of us is writing? Neither can we.

We're writing this because speaking *money* is like speaking any language. If you don't speak at least a little of it, you can't travel there, and you can't eat the food. You certainly can't do business there. You can fall in love with someone who speaks a different language but, frankly, that's overrated (Ali wrote that!). Ironically, while you may speak the same *language* as the people closest to you, not speaking money could cause you as much grief as trying to read this book in French (which Christine, ironically, can do).

Speak money, and your world will open up. You'll have fewer fights, fewer fears, and you'll catch more opportunities. You'll have less anxiety, and you'll be better equipped to make the most of what you have, what you earn, and what you can attain in the future.

Because this is a book about speaking a language, we'll take you on a tour of the world of money, allowing you to speak it intelligently and confidently. You'll discover how you can build a better future for yourself, even if your present is less than wonderful. Even if you're not disciplined by nature, we'll teach you how a few simple techniques can keep you on the right track.

We've organized the book so that it flows logically, in a series of chapters that take you from the personal (your relationships, your gender) to the broader world in which you live. We don't agree on everything, but we both agree that you need to understand and master the language of money to unlock the best opportunities of the coming decade. We also agree that we (society, America, the media) obsess about the domestic economy, when we'd be better served to understand it in the context of the global marketplace.

Going through *How to Speak Money* chapter by chapter, here's what you'll find:

Chapter 1: The Big Picture: This is where we lay out a lot of the themes that we'll spend the rest of the book helping you understand. Think of it as the "Why you need to speak money" chapter.

Chapter 2: *We* Fight About Money, Too: We are economic snowflakes. No two of us feel exactly the same about money, even if we share a background. And that's okay. We argue our points with one another. We explain to each other what matters to us and why. At the end we reach an agreement, or a compromise, or one of us gives in—this time—with the tacit understanding that next time—or the next time—the other one gets to win.

More relationships break up over money than over any other issue. So learning how to discuss it, and why it's okay to feel differently about it than your significant other may feel, is pretty important.

Chapter 3: Gendernomics: Folks speak money differently for different reasons, and one of them is gender. History has assigned different economic roles to men and women and while *most* of those lines have been blurred, many people still identify with them, and struggle with breaking out of preconceived ideas and roles. Remember *I Love Lucy*, where men guarded the checkbook while women just couldn't wait to run out and buy new clothes? We know that's largely not true anymore, but we've recently reported on some stunning neuroeconomic research that measures the brain activity of men and women in response to different risk/reward situations. Turns out we are wired a little differently and by understanding how we're wired, we can adapt our behavior more effectively. Both men and women have emotional impulses that we can override to deal with our financial lives in a more rational and objective way.

Chapter 4: Speaking Money around the World: You know there's a trend that's reshaping the world's economic structure: globalization. It's exemplified by the rise of China, and it's permanently altered our way of doing business. You can't hope to get fluent in money without understanding how to take advantage of (or, depending on your perspective, protect yourself from) this new paradigm. Believe us: it's personal. The changes globalization have brought have profound implications for every American. They have an impact on our educational and career choices, they influence our mortgage rates and, while they certainly shake our comfort zones, they also offer tremendous opportunity.

Christine earned an Emmy award covering the impact of globalization on American workers. From her perspective, the world changes so quickly that a worker's skills can't keep up under normal conditions. Ali's view is influenced by the CEOs and businesspeople he interviews who see rapid transformation—and huge potential—in the way business is conducted, and by the people he's met in the thousand of miles he traveled on the CNN Express during the recession. Together, we give you the information you need to take advantage of the many new possibilities in our interconnected world.

Chapter 5: Speaking Money at Work: You can live without your investments going up in value, and you can live without owning a house. But unless you marry rich, rob a bank, or win the lottery, you need an income. And that's the same in any language. Christine and Ali probably spend more time following employment trends in the United States and elsewhere than they do on anything else, because if you can answer the employment puzzle, everything else follows. What industries will offer the best growth prospects? What kind of salary can you expect? What if you're just starting out? What if you need to change direction at age 40? We'll cover all that and more in our section on career choices. Most importantly, we show you how to identify promising areas that align with your skills and interests.

Chapter 6: Speaking Money on Campus: Not that we disagree on this, but enough people seem to disagree with us that we've devoted a chapter to it. Read our lips: A university education is the single best defense against unemployment. Period. We'll show you the courses of study that will land you in the best position to succeed. And what about community colleges, three-year programs, graduate school, and vocational training? It's all education, but is it all valuable? The answers will help you make the best possible choices for you or your kid, and not go broke in the process.

Chapter 7: Speaking Money in the Market: The goal of becoming fluent in money is to build wealth over time. Today, there are more investment options than ever before. There are also risks that didn't exist before. From bank deposits and CDs to stocks, bonds, mutual funds, and ETFs, there are investment and savings vehicles to suit the risk and reward specifications of every investor. We look at them all, and show you how to choose the best ones for you.

Chapter 8: Speaking Money to Investment Principles: Once you know what's out there, we explain the basic principles of successful investing and show you how to find the approach that's best for your situation.

Chapter 9: Speaking Money with Your Own Portfolio: By blending different asset classes, you can improve the likelihood of achieving your goals. We've even prepared model portfolios for a variety of objectives, and a self-test to help you determine which might be most appropriate for you.

Chapter 10: Speaking Money on the Home Front: Whether it's your spouse, your kids, your parents, your roommate, or your siblings, sometimes it feels like you're not speaking in the same language group, never mind language. Love is not the best translator, and blood isn't thicker than financial misunderstanding. So why not please read at least *this* chapter *before* making the biggest investment you are *ever* likely to make? Wherever you live, you're going to have to pay for the privilege, either with a rent check or a mortgage payment. Which one is better for you? We'll show you.

Chapter 11: Speaking Money on Budget (or how *not* to end up like the U.S. government): Ali's not that familiar with budgeting, so Christine's going to take the lead on this chapter ☺. Seriously, while you're building that nest egg we talked about in Chapters 7, 8, and 9, and saving up for the home in Chapter 10, you've got bills to pay! Ali wants you to invest to get rich, but Christine warns you can't even *think* about that until you understand the relationship between what you take in and what you spend, intimately. In our chapter on budgeting, we'll show you how to establish and monitor a realistic spending plan so that you don't bleed excess cash. Ask anyone who's ever been on a diet: They'll tell you that one of the most important tools for staying on track is to keep a record of every bite they consume. Replace every bite you consume with every dollar you spend, and you'll understand why having a budget is so important to building wealth. It brings discipline to what would otherwise be a haphazard process. If you're not going to take it seriously, there's no point in doing it at all.

Chapter 12: Speaking Money in Retirement: At the end, we discuss retirement. For many it's a distant, indistinct vision; to others it's so close it's blurry. A surprising number of Americans think it's okay not to have your retirement funds in place because you can always work a few years longer. But unless you're the boss, that may not be your call. While Social Security provides some income, it's not enough to cover all your living costs. If you want to live comfortably later—no matter how far away "later" is, buckle down and get a strategy now. If you get this far in the book, you can consider yourself fluent in the language of money.

At the end of this book, we want you to be more confident, more assured, more knowledgeable and more in control of your financial life. We want you to be completely fluent in money, able to handle the day-to-day conversations about finances, and able to translate your knowledge into planning competent strategies for building wealth and retirement savings.

CHAPTER 1

The Big Picture

For several years now, money has dominated the national conversation. Our CNN/ORC polling first put the economy as "Issue Number 1" back in December of 2007. From the financial crisis in 2008, to the Great Recession that ended in late 2009, to the job drought that followed—virtually every headline that matters to your family's well-being has been about money.

America is downgraded. The unemployment rate is stubbornly high. Congress fights about how to spend your money, and the nation's debt and deficits grow and grow.

China's economy is soaring. Emerging markets are on fire. Europe has a debt crisis. State and local governments are closing parks, raising fees, firing teachers. More than a quarter of all homeowners owe more on their home than the home is worth.

What's going on with gold? Stocks have been a nervous wreck and bond yields have reached record lows.

Oh yeah, and the Fed has pumped trillions of dollars into the banking system to grease the economy.

What does all this mean?

Parlez-vous anxiety?

Need a job? Have one but want a promotion? You need to speak money to understand that every hire is about a boss making a financial decision. Want your child to find a good career? You need to speak money to choose a college and a major that won't bankrupt your family or saddle the kid with debt. Want to just keep your money safe in the bank? You need to speak money to make sure your friendly neighborhood banker isn't siphoning away your hard-earned cash through needless fees.

Maybe your money problem is not having enough of it. Or maybe you have no idea how much it will take to retire, because you are just trying to make the money last the month. Or maybe you are just down-right angry that the money seems to flow on Wall Street but Main Street is hurting. And maybe, just maybe, you have the unsettling concern that America's best days are behind her.

It may sound harsh. But you can't afford not to learn this language.

We're not advocating the blind pursuit of material things and financial success. Au contraire. We're just saying you need to understand all of this happening with urgency around you, so that someone else's blind pursuit of money doesn't hurt you and you can live the life you deserve.

What does it mean to be fluent in money? It means following all of these conversations—about college, jobs, debt, deficits, and politics—and translating what it means for your family.

We want you to make your family and your world a better place. Cheesy? Yes. Possible? Absolutely.

Money Is Everywhere

Whether you think it is crass or greedy to admit it, the fact is money is the world's global language.

Being fluent in money affects every area of your life. It's more than simply your savings or the investments you may have.

It's about the way you spend it, save it, invest it, use it, need it, and want it. Your financial life includes your house, your job, your family's education, your monthly budget, your retirement planning, and your credit cards. It's about your ability to defer pleasure versus your desire for instant gratification. It's how you decide whether to take that vacation, buy that furniture, or go out to dinner versus using that same money to build your nest egg, save for retirement, or fund your kids' college education.

It's also about how you vote and what you expect from your government, because guess what—your elected officials may not speak money with the same accent you do!

The two of us speak money every day for our job, trying to translate what is happening in the halls of Congress, the boardrooms of corporate America, and the humming ports of China. These stories are connected to your everyday life; of that, we are certain. The culture of commerce is everywhere, and it affects your interest rates, your job prospects, and your retirement hopes.

There's very little information that doesn't have something to do with money. Whether it's a drought in far-off western China or a two-year redevelopment plan on a busy street in your town, these events can have a meaningful impact on your life and on your finances. It's certain that they'll affect you. If you know how to speak money, you'll be able to take advantage of them.

That drought in China? If the lack of water means that the Chinese can't grow enough grain to feed their own people, they'll be forced to buy food from other countries. That will push up worldwide prices for wheat, corn, and rice, and everyone will feel the pain at the checkout counter in the form of higher grocery bills. But at the same time, those who are fluent in money might invest in a commodity fund that positions them to capitalize on the rising price of basic foodstuffs.

As for the redevelopment plan in your town, watch what happens in the early stages, when jackhammers and bulldozers start ripping up the street. As sidewalks narrow and dust fills the air, retail businesses close and property values fall. People prefer not to shop or eat in the midst of a major construction project; and no one wants to live on a street that sounds like a war zone. But when all is completed, money comes back to an improved neighborhood. The streets look better. The buildings have new facades and they appear more upscale. Those who were able to wait out the process—or who bought in during the active phase—find their stores and homes are now worth more.

We also acknowledge that people approach money differently and use money to express themselves in an almost infinite number of ways. Just like us, two people can have different wants, needs, and expectations from money. Speaking money in your personal relationships also means understanding where your friend/partner/spouse/co-worker/kid is coming from and knowing there is no wrong answer.

To be fluent in money, you have to use it to express your own thoughts and your own wants and needs. You have to give it your own spin, just as you speak English (or whatever language you speak) with your own individual vocabulary, accent, and syntax.

Understanding Money

As commercial and trade barriers have fallen, money has taken on a decidedly international flavor. We now have access to opportunities in countries that were formerly not sufficiently developed to deliver the requisite transparency and verifiable information that investors demand. Schools now teach skills that will enable us to land jobs in almost any country on Earth. While the pace of change is obliterating certain ways of working, it's also creating new careers with outstanding growth potential for those with the foresight and commitment to take them.

At the same time that the world is becoming increasingly money-fluent, money is becoming more intimate as well. We're learning more about basic, fundamental differences between men and women; differences that affect their approaches to wealth building, budgeting, and planning.

The thing is, everyone speaks it differently. That's among the factors that make money such a fascinating language. Ali sees a stock market decline of 635 points, and is instantly scouring the S&P 500 for potential growth sectors. Christine sees the same decline, and thinks first of how many more months of working it will take to fill up the college savings fund again.

You can't speak any language—money included—without understanding some basic principles. You have to know the nouns, the verbs, the rules for conjugation, where the modifiers go, and more. Understanding these things is easy in languages we've heard from birth; but it can be more difficult when we're learning one for the first time. With any luck, though, money isn't completely foreign to you—you may just need a refresher course.

Nouns, as we all remember from junior high school, are names of people, places, and things. (There are also what are called abstract nouns: honor, duty, friendship, and so forth; but this is a financial book, not an English lesson.) In the world of money, nouns name the areas of your financial life and the products that can help you achieve your goals. They include words like *budget, education, investments, career,* and others.

Money verbs—action words—include *study, apply, buy, sell, hold, trade, train,* and many more that describe steps you take to secure a better future for yourself and your family. We could go on to draw analogies for adjectives, adverbs, conjunctions, prepositions, and even expletives, but really . . . enough already.

Where Are You?

The other parts of money you need to know are the grammatical rules that guide putting the various words together. This begins by understanding where you are in the life-building process. The steps that a college student should take are different from those recommended for a 35-year-old. A married mother of two must chart a different course from the path chosen by a single, unattached male. A couple nearing retirement has neither the requirements—nor the range of options—of a couple in its prime earning years.

What are the biggest impediments to obtaining the life you want? The life you need? The obstacles fall into two categories: external and internal. The external factors include the big, macroeconomic shifts taking place around the world. You can't influence them any more than you can affect an approaching hurricane. The best you can do is to understand them and deal with them.

The internal factors, though, are completely under your control. These include how much money you spend, how much you save, and how you position yourself for success in a changing world. If a storm is coming, then a storm is coming: You can't change that. But if a storm is coming and you don't prepare for it—if you don't close your windows, put batteries in the flashlight, and put the car in the garage—then the damage is likely to be your own fault.

Neither you, nor your spouse, children, parents, boyfriend, girlfriend, roommate(s), partner, significant other, dog, cat, or goldfish is responsible for the Great Recession. You're not responsible for jobs lost in the American manufacturing sector or the budget deficit. If you own a home, you're not responsible for it perhaps being worth less today than it was when you bought it. (That is, unless you bought it with an interest-only loan with no money down and fudged your income in the loan process. We can't help you with that.)

But you *are* responsible for the way in which you respond to these realities. Complaining is not an action plan. Blaming the universe won't help you fix things. You need to move forward despite the unfairness. Life is tough: You must be tougher.

So we're going to give you a series of language lessons to help you understand those previously foreign areas of your life. You'll see how to live below your means so that you can put money away for the future. You'll learn what jobs offer the best growth prospects, and where those jobs are located. You'll understand that globalization—among the most feared words in the lexicon—need not be a threat; it can be an opportunity. And you'll discover that, no matter what your age, you can start making it better.

Getting to Where You Want to Go

The first order of business is to understand *who* you are and *where* you are. What do you like? Can you narrow it down? What's your appetite for risk? How much do you know about investments? Do you live on a budget? Are you a planner? Are you disciplined? How old are you? Do you have a family or are you unattached? None of these markers say much in and of themselves, but collectively they can help you open profitable doors and close the drafty ones.

If you're young enough to still be in school, then the world is your oyster. True, jobs aren't as plentiful right now as they were in the mid-2000s, but you can still pursue a course of study that will lead you to an in-demand career. If you're somewhat older, perhaps engaged in a career that doesn't seem as rewarding as it once did, maybe it's time to consider transitioning into a field more in line with your talents and expectations.

If you're nearing retirement, or wondering how you're ever going to retire, let's look at the careers and life opportunities that would benefit from the experience you've accumulated in your years on Planet Earth. Remember, you're in charge of your own life. You have choices. Only you can judge which choice will be most satisfying for you. Our job is to lay out the options, provide guidelines, offer our perspective as professional financial journalists, and let you know that you're not alone in this effort.

We don't want you to be afraid of money when you're talking with your family, with your boss, with your credit card company, or with a prospective employer. We want to make sure that you're comfortable enough with the basics of this material to take the next step and start building wealth on your own. Instead of being defensive about financial issues, we want you to be assertive enough to get your money to work for you.

When you boil it down, we're all looking for comfort and happiness. Each of us may define those things differently, but money is the common tool that makes them possible. We can't say it enough: Please understand that we're not talking about the race to acquire a lot of money, because that's not what we're about. We just want to make sure that you're not sabotaging yourself by not knowing how to speak the language.

At the end of the race that we call life, the people who are successful and comfortable are the people who made sure they had a cushion there. That cushion brings a pretty significant sense of calm, and it gives you the freedom to pursue other things that make you happy.

In our 10 years of working together as financial reporters, we've observed trends, fads, bubbles, and troughs. We've seen bull markets and bear markets, and we've seen conditions that were good, bad, and—recently—quite ugly. Our takeaway is simple: There are no shortcuts to success; there are no get-rich-quick schemes that work. Success takes planning, discipline, and dedication. Wishing is not a strategy.

But the good part is that the steps you need to take are really not so difficult. They're logical and doable. Once you begin to learn the language, each subsequent step is easier. Once you start to move forward, you build momentum quickly. As Isaac Newton put it some 350 years ago, "A body in motion tends to stay in motion." That body can be yours.

Getting Started

You know more about money than you think you do. There is an intimidation factor that exists with money that doesn't exist in other areas of our life. But we are here to tell you that you make important decisions every day without necessarily thinking that they are money decisions. For example, so many decisions about education are ultimately, financial decisions. Your kid gets a bad report card, and earns from you a week grounded from the cell phone. That is a financial decision—you are angry about the grade because of what it means for his future college and job prospects. And the grounding is powerful incentive to change the behavior by denying the kid a reward that has financial value he relies on. Even what you eat for lunch is a financial decision. That's why lunch specials do so well.

Christine loves cucumbers and celery at the company salad bar. Ali likes to remind her that those are the worst return on her lunch money. Sun-dried tomatoes and beets, believe it or not, are more valuable per ounce.

But most people aren't like us, weighing just about everything as a financial transaction.

We don't recommend obsessing about the relative value of sesame seeds versus bacon bits, but we do think too many people get bogged down in the details of their financial life at the expense of the overall picture.

Mapping a coherent strategy can be difficult. We often see people who have painstakingly paid off debt to improve their credit score, only to borrow too much money again, reverting to the old ways that started the problem in the first place without getting even a step closer to more retirement money.

So you need to define your needs and wants (two different things), relate them to your position in life, and then—and only then—map out a plan to make the two conform to each other.

Most people pick up whatever they know about money haphazardly. Very few of us grow up reading the *Wall Street Journal*. Not that many of us have parents who educated us about saving and investing, about making financial choices, about budgeting. It's ironic that there's more emphasis on sex education than financial education in our public schools.

Life costs money. That's why you need to understand your finances.

—*Thomas Wynbrandt, American author and songwriter*

What we know tends to come from experience. Some of us work through high school; more of us work in college; and all of us (we hope) find jobs and enter the working world after we finish our formal educations. But while we may know what it means to pick up a paycheck and to pay our bills, fewer of us understand how to structure a financial plan that will help us build for the future.

To fill the gap, some of us hire financial advisors. We nod along and pretend to be knowledgeable when they present us with their strategies, all the while hoping they know what they're doing. Because not only don't we know enough to develop our own plans, we don't know enough to evaluate the ones they've prepared for us.

Our secondary schools should do a better job of making students financially literate. Every student should know about interest rates, investment categories, the difference between good debt and bad debt, the power of compound interest, and all the other subjects that, when understood, can help them make the right choices to gain control over their financial lives.

In today's world, speaking money is a basic survival skill (have you been watching the news?), just as important as knowing how to drive a car or send a text message.

The truth is, it's never too early and it's never too late to begin saving and investing your money. And just about every decision you make is a step toward that goal.

The Key to Wealth: Live Below Your Means

We've all heard stories of people who lived beyond their means. Just a few years ago it was very easy to do—rising real estate prices meant that just about everyone could borrow against the value of their home and have a good time with the money: ritzy vacations, giant hi-def televisions, fancy cars—you name it. But with the crash and the attendant recession, that kind of extravagance (And frankly, some lived beyond their means to pay for college tuition and medical bills—extravagant no, but a dangerous position to be in.) became not just obnoxious, but impossible. Many of those people lost everything, including the homes that fueled their behavior in the first place.

The smart thing to do is to live *below* your means, and to put the money you don't spend to work for you. How? By investing it. Your choice of investment vehicle is up to you, but the basic principle—putting your money to work—is constant.

Most everyone feels they're already doing all they can. And most everyone turns out to be a little bit wrong. To get a real handle on your spending, you must have a budget. A real budget. A budget that tracks every dollar you spend on everything: housing, transportation, food, entertainment, laundry, clothing, tips, pets, kids, lottery tickets (a poor strategy for building wealth, but a strategy nonetheless)—everything.

In each category of expenses, there are probably creative ways to reduce your costs and free up some funds you can then put to work. Not all of these creative solutions will square with your idea of a Cliff Huxtable household, but they will work, and that's the important thing.

Living below your means is the one character constant we've observed in all the successful CEOs we've ever interviewed. Many of them are naturally frugal, unimpressed by the showier trappings of wealth. Some had frugality forced on them by circumstance, and they found the discipline beneficial. A few others we've covered over the years lived to the max, the equivalent of the ugly American on the demure streets of Paris. Many of those are serving time. But hey, that's probably just a coincidence.

Change with the Times

More and more, we're seeing people adapt to changing circumstance in ways that are innovative, intelligent, and heretofore uncommon. Take housing, for example. Many families have added an extra generation to the household. When Grandma or Grandpa (or both) move in, they help with the rent, help with the kids (a major plus in a household with two working parents) and they no longer have to carry the expense of their own residence, freeing up money for the extended family as a single unit.

This won't work for everyone, but the pursuit of financial independence often requires a few sacrifices. And let's not forget that multiple generations under one roof was the norm in this country (and in all societies) not that long ago. Most families who have tried it say the benefits go far beyond the financial. They say it builds a sense of closeness and unity that is emotionally satisfying for all members of the household.

Food is another area in which it's possible to economize. Cutting back on restaurant meals is the easiest step. Cutting back on takeout is next. The third step is to be a more careful shopper. Buy non-perishable items in bulk. Use coupons—their use has soared in the past two years. Take advantage of flash sales on Groupon and other social networking sites. Your savings can be significant.

Start putting your money into different buckets. We did a story recently on a 14-year-old Florida boy who already has four separate bank accounts. One is his savings account, one is his checking account, one is his college fund, and one holds the money he'll use to buy a car when he's old enough to drive it. The young man puts at least $10 into the bank each week. That's the kind of consistency and discipline we'd all do well to emulate.

By dividing your money into different pools, depending on what you want it to do for you, you're doing more than just accumulating it—you're giving it a purpose. It makes it easier to save, because the reason you're saving is more concrete. If you're saving for a car, for example, you can feel that car coming closer with each deposit you make. If you're planning for a new kitchen, having a new-kitchen account will make that item increasingly real for you, spurring your efforts to reach the goal more quickly. (That said, our reporting has shown that a kitchen renovation is an expensive investment that will not return all of your money. Perhaps you should consider a "new siding" or a "new insulated garage doors" fund instead. People fluent in money are making those investments. Until the housing market improves, we are not ready to recommend a fancy kitchen renovation as a good investment. But if you want a new kitchen because it makes you happy and you can afford it, we hear ya. Go right ahead.)

It's Up to You

One more word of advice: Don't expect help from anyone. Assume you're going to have to do it all on your own. It would be nice if you had a support staff, but you don't. Take charge of your life. When you do that, you're learning how to speak money.

We live in difficult economic times, and it doesn't appear that they're going to get much easier anytime soon. That's why you need this book. You need to be able to speak money in order to live your life well.

Here's how we'll do it. We've divided the book into 12 chapters, each of them dealing with a different area of your financial life. We're writing the book together—Ali and Christine, Christine and Ali. But just because we're writing it together doesn't mean we agree on everything all the time. No two people do. So where we disagree, we're going to give you both points of view. Neither is wrong; it's simply that there's more than one way to be right.

In fact, that's one of the most important things to understand about speaking money: It's personal. Your decisions have to be right for the person you are. Ultimately, you're the only one who knows how important that car, that vacation, or that TV is to you.

Only you can decide whether the pleasure you'll get from a given purchase outweighs the potential value of that same amount of money if you invest it instead.

Again, it's your life. You should build it so that it's satisfying to you. We can (and will) give you the tools, and we can (and will) show you how to use them. But what you create is strictly your call.

Different Strokes, Different Folks

The person you are is a combination of your genetic makeup and the experiences you've had. Those experiences start with home life and expand as you get older to incorporate more of the wide world around you. For us—Christine and Ali—our differences are completely understandable in light of our dissimilar backgrounds.

Making Your Plan

There are no short cuts in getting where you want to go. But, fortunately, there are paths you can follow that will lead you to your

How to Speak Money—*Talking Points*

Ali says

My father, my grandfather, and my uncle were business people in South Africa. They ran a big industrial bakery there. They were also anti-apartheid activists. When the government began to crack down on their political activities, my mother and father decided to leave. My father was 25, my mother was 18, and my sister had just been born.

They moved to Kenya. My father opened another bakery and he ultimately landed in real estate. Then I was born. Eventually, my parents felt the political situation there wasn't stable enough for the long term. So when I was one-and-a-half, we all moved to Canada, where I grew up.

At an early age—I think I was 12—I began investing in stocks. I loved to get the newspaper and check the price of the stocks I owned. It was the same way some kids check baseball stats, only much nerdier.

Being only 12, my stock-picking methodology wasn't very sophisticated. But I wanted to learn, and a few years later I had a stockbroker and we would talk about various companies. In retrospect, he must have been quite amused. I was barely 15.

How to Speak Money—*Talking Points*

Christine says

I grew up in Iowa, the granddaughter of farmers, a profession among the riskiest in the world. In the best of times, farmers deal with shifting variables and unrelenting uncertainty.

You are always at the mercy of the weather. If it doesn't rain, it rains too much. If there is hail or pests or drought or flood, it will wipe you out. A broken tractor part at the peak of planting or harvest is an immediate cash nightmare.

Even deciding what to plant—corn, soybeans, wheat, maybe try cotton this year since it is forecast to be dry?—is fraught with huge financial implications. Some farmers owe the bank for the seeds, for the note on the combine, for the trucks, for just about everything else.

Then there is another kind of farmer—incredibly risk averse. That was us. My maternal grandparents paid cash. They planted one year with the profit from the last. That was passed down to me. My dad's folks were equally careful with money. Their cultural references were the sinking of the *Titanic* and the Great Depression—both exercises in risk run amok. These were powerful influences for a little girl.

destination. Our friend Bruce Sellery, a very successful financial expert and best-selling author, laid out a five-step program in his book, *Moolala*. The steps are easy and straightforward, and they make a lot of sense.

1. *Lay the foundation.* Answer the question, "What's my money for?" In truth, it's for everything—it's for experiences, it's for living, it's for contributions, family, stuff, and wild cards. So understand what you need from your money. Once you answer that question, you can take a deep breath and start to relax. You're on your way. Because once you've identified your interests, it's much more likely that you'll make the responsible decisions, rather than buying the Jimmy Choos or the Rolex.
2. *Determine what you want.* There's a big difference between "retirement" and "living in a villa in Tuscany" or "getting a master's degree in French Literature." One is vague and boring; the others are specific and exciting. The more you

visualize exactly what you want your future to be, the easier it will be to achieve it. (This concept of visualization, by the way, is exactly the discipline used by star athletes to reach their full potential.)

3. *Develop a plan for your money.* It's funny. People develop plans to lose weight; they adhere to a plan at the gym; they'll develop a plan to launch a product at work; but when it comes to their finances, they're often lost in space. That won't cut it. Figure out what it will take to get you to your goal.

4. *Take action on your plan.* We're a procrastinating species. And when we realize we haven't done anything, we ask ourselves, "Why haven't I taken action on my plan?" Well, there are likely a million reasons. And while they may all be legitimate, they don't really matter. So the question we should be asking is, "What will it take to get me to take action?" It may be creativity, patience, discipline, courage, or a combination of them. But you've got deep reservoirs of each of those qualities. Don't be afraid to move forward.

5. *Stay engaged.* Wouldn't it be great if you could fill your refrigerator one time and it would stay full for the rest of your life? Needless to say, it doesn't work that way. You have to keep on top of it. It's the same with your money. If you don't keep control of your financial life, the future will just happen to you. You deserve better.

 How to Speak Money's Words to the Wise

1. Self-awareness (*sel•fa•wair'•niss*): Know your own mind. Only you know what will make you happy. Only you know where you want to be in 3, 5, 10, or even 20 years. Once you define your individual goals, you can then begin planning to reach them.

2. Big Picture (*big•pik'•sh'r*): Don't get so caught up in the details of money management that you neglect the large, strategic issues that are most important to your future. You need to look at the whole forest, not the individual trees.

3. Under-spend (*un•d'r•spend'*): Live below your means. The less you spend now, the more you'll have to invest for later. It takes discipline and focus, but spending less than you earn is the only sure path to growth.

CHAPTER 2

We Fight About Money, Too

Talking about money, even between friends and spouses, has become one of the most difficult conversations in America. Why this should be so has any number of explanations: It's rarely a pleasant talk (it's generally akin to showing a bad report card to your parents); it goes to the heart of who we are; all our values are wrapped up in it; it's fertile ground for disagreement; and the news has been so bad, there really isn't a happy conversation about money these days. No one we know has ever started a financial discussion by saying, "We have way too much money and we're not spending nearly enough."

So these are not blithe chats. But we must talk about money, candidly and regularly, if we're to hack our way through our collective defenses and get to the pure, molten heart of the issue. And the issue is: Money cannot be ignored.

Parents know their children are the most important things in the world. That's why you raise your children. You watch over them and care for them. You guide and nurture them. Their future is important. Well, your future is important, too. You must raise your money as carefully as you would your kids.

In many ways, it's easier. Money won't talk back, won't engage in inappropriate behavior, and won't stay out late and forget to call you. It will do exactly what you tell it to do while obeying the laws of the economy and the market.

Money, though, is an arena in which our deepest hopes and fears are expressed in symbolic form. Some people find it physically

15

painful to part with money. (Christine.) Others can't wait to spend it. (Ali.) For some, accumulating money in the bank brings welcome feelings of security and peace. Others seek the emotional high they get with the purchase of a new gadget or a new handbag.

We bring so much baggage to discussions of money that Douglas K. Flynn, a New York–based certified financial planner and a principal at Flynn Zito LLC, told us, "We often joke that we should have a couch in our office, because once people start opening up about money, then it all comes out."

In courtship, the most important money discussions rarely take place before people commit to one another. "When you're thinking about getting married or becoming a significant other," Flynn said, "Do you know what kind of person you are? Do you know what kind of person the other person is? People don't seem equipped to have these conversations."

Or maybe they just don't want to know.

Stacy Francis, principal of Francis Financial, a financial planning firm in New York City, echoes Flynn's thoughts.

"Unfortunately," she said, "Many couples don't talk about money before they get married. They have no idea that their partner has $50,000 in credit card debt until they get married and they go to buy their first home together.

"Money is an issue that many people are worried to talk about. Either they don't want to offend someone, or they worry that a person is not going to love them because they have a spending issue, or whatever. They're much more willing to talk about sex," she said.

So it's pretty clear that while discussions of money between two consenting adults is not exactly taboo, there are many obstacles to bringing it out in the open.

The problem is the value judgments that we fear others will assign to our money habits. If I enjoy shopping, does it mean that I'm shallow, weak, frivolous, arrogant, or highfalutin? If I prefer to put my money in the bank rather than part with it, does it make me a tightwad, a Scrooge, a stick-in-the-mud, or cruel? It's odd that in this day and age, when we're encouraged to be who we are in so many areas of life, that we worry so about how others will interpret our money habits.

So be who you are. And understand, as Stacy Francis, put it, "Every person has a different financial DNA. Each person has an individual approach to dealing with and spending money."

She noted that, "Money is a part of every piece of your life. The money histories that we each have—that created us and formed us, that really molded our behaviors and our beliefs about ourselves and about money—were formed so long ago. It's not something that you can undo very easily."

In other words, our money behaviors aren't something that's added on to us; they're an outward expression of who we are at the core.

A Failure to Communicate

It might seem like a little white lie that doesn't hurt anyone—hiding a credit card, downplaying your debt to your significant other, even lying just a little about how much you make.

But love and money experts agree—too much debt and frequent disagreements about money can be disastrous. Like everything in a relationship, communication is key.

Many behaviors can have a negative impact on a couple's relationship:

- Hiding debt: Some bring huge debts into the relationship and hide them.
- Resent spending: Sometimes savers resent their spouse's spending.
- Revenge shopping: Sometimes a spouse secretly spends for revenge, or to display independence.

So the question is, if you're telling little white lies about your money, does that show you don't trust your spouse or are you worried your spouse won't trust you?

Jacquette Timmons, the author of *Financial Intimacy*, told us, "If you are afraid to talk about money, what else are you not discussing in your relationship?

The key issue? "It's trust. It's never just about the money. It's about what's revealed as a result of that."

According to a survey from *Forbes Woman* and the National Endowment for Financial Education, 31 percent of Americans who have combined their finances say they've lied to their spouse about money. Sixty-seven percent of that group said their behavior caused arguments. And 16 percent broke up as a result.

Not surprisingly, many of those lies are about debt, a potential marriage destroyer. A certain amount of debt is quite common in today's lives, but too much suggests we're out of control. And that's not good.

Research from Utah State University shows that thrifty couples are happiest and too much debt can ruin a marriage.

Jeffrey Dew, a Utah State University professor, states it clearly: "Couples with consumer debt tend to fight more, they are more stressed about their money, and some recent research that I have done even shows that consumer debt is associated with divorce."

Dew says that a couple with $10,000 in debt and no savings is about twice as likely to divorce as a couple with $10,000 in savings and no credit card debt.

"When your savings can take the financial pressure off, then couples are able to focus on each other rather than on the financial problems that they have," he added.

If you have debt, you're going to need both patience and a plan. You'll likely be going through some stress.

Jacquette Timmons notes, "It's going to put a spotlight on how well you communicate. Do you share the same values? Do you have the same goals?"

The only thing that will get you through is communication. Open, honest communication. The good news is that communication, at least, is free.

How Do You Have a Difficult Conversation?

There are probably as many ways for couples to talk about money as there are relationships. But not all are equally effective. Simply dropping the checkbook and a stack of bills on your partner's lap when she is watching television, for example, might not be the best approach.

Some couples have financial dates. Once a month, they get a baby sitter, go out, have a glass of wine and go over what the spending was for that month. They review their savings, their 401(k)s, their 529 plans, and the emergency account, to see if they hit their goals. Because they're working jointly toward common goals, these dates not only address the immediate purpose of the evening, they tend to strengthen the bonds between the couple as well.

The tenor of their evening brings up another critical point. In discussions with someone you love, it's important to come from a place of honor and respect, not, "I'm right and you're wrong." There are many valid points of view, since right and wrong are relative terms here. Money, as we've seen, is a highly charged issue. Your goal should be setting your relationship on a solid financial foundation; your goal should not be to win an argument.

The only thing money gives you is the freedom of not worrying about money.

> —*Johnny Carson, late-night television host*

Doug Flynn sees this dynamic played out every day in his role as a financial planner. Usually, he says, couples are driven to his office by a feeling that they need to gain more control over their financial affairs rather than a pursuit of any individual objective.

"Retirement's always up there," he said. "Putting the kids through college is always up there. Often, it's about buying homes and second homes and stuff like that. But it's really about getting a handle on what a couple needs in order to have the lifestyle they want. What is it that they need to do?"

Argue Box

Christine says

I hate to part with money. I'm very deliberate in my decisions and it can take me a long time to make them. When the recession hit a couple of years ago, it was all I could do to not take my money and hide it under my mattress. Knowing money is there gives me a feeling of peace. It's one of the reasons I admire entrepreneurs and risk takers who can swallow their unease and make a bold move to grow wealth. Caution is in my DNA!

Ali says

I'm a terrible saver. That's why I need my money to make money for me. When the recession hit, I stayed with my plan. I kept my money invested, did some rebalancing and let the market take its course. That strategy paid off, as it always has.

Flynn assists these couples in developing plans that will work for them. Often, his simply being a neutral facilitator rather than someone with a stake in the outcome helps the couples reach decisions they might not have achieved on their own.

"Once they understand, 'If I do this and I put my kids through school and after I do that, I can retire comfortably,' then they can go home and spend the rest of that money because they're covering what they need to do. The problem is that most people don't have unlimited funds, and they have to make choices. How do you spread your wealth? Where do you apply the money? It's not a matter of us dictating goals. It's a matter of the couple determining which goals are most important to them."

These are discussions you need to have in your own household. What goals *are* most important to you? How much are you willing to sacrifice to attain them? What's your tolerance for pain? How much will it hurt to take a *stay*cation instead of a *va*cation? Conversely, will you be able to enjoy a night on the town if you're feeling guilty about the more prudent ways in which that money could have been used?

Perhaps we're being too harsh in trying to dish out a bit of tough love. The truth is that speaking money in your relationship and following through on the plans you make needn't be the financial equivalent of a forced march.

Once each of you realizes where the other is coming from, it may be easier to give yourself—and your other—individual comfort space while still respecting the overall mission.

One couple we know resolved their spending arguments through the use of three accounts: one for him, one for her, and a joint account for their family finances. He, the spender, used to dip into their joint savings to buy the gadgets and gizmos that made him feel up to the minute. She, the saver, treasured her weekly massages and not much else. The discrepancy in their spending patterns was a lightning rod for trouble.

Now, each of them has a monthly allowance, placed into their individual accounts, to be spent in any fashion they choose, no questions asked. The allowance is not a significant sum, but it's enough to let each of them afford the small indulgences that make their lives more pleasurable.

Yes, he has occasionally spent his entire allowance before the month was out and then asked for money from his wife's account; but she's refused. He's respected her decision. A deal's a deal.

Three Keys to a Meaningful Financial Conversation

1. Take the initiative (someone has to do it).
2. Be honest with your partner.
3. Be honest with yourself.

That last item, be honest with yourself, is a very important one. Sometimes we say that we don't talk money because we don't want to provoke an argument. But maybe it's really because we don't want to face up to our own financial responsibilities. Maybe as long as we can blame the other, either out loud or in our own minds, for the fact that our savings are lagging, that we haven't done what we said we'd do, that we bought that thing we wanted but knew we couldn't afford—then we don't have to look in the mirror and point the finger at ourselves. It may be better to light a candle than to curse the darkness; but the latter activity is much easier.

The objective of a couple's frank and constructive (to use the diplomatic term) discussions isn't to make you into someone you're not; it's to find a way to be who you are in the context of a relationship, with the understanding that not all gratification can be instantaneous.

Doug Flynn notes that in a successful relationship, "Someone takes the saver role and someone takes the spender role." That's true even if neither is a true saver nor spender. It's simply that relative to each other, one will be more a spender or saver than the other.

Flynn continued, "I've had men savers and women spenders and vice versa. It's not a gender thing. All I know is that the most successful marriages have one and the other. They balance each other, and striking the balance is the goal."

In a regard to who in a relationship initiates a financial discussion, Flynn offered an analogy: "If one of the kids throws his shirt at the hamper and it doesn't make it in and it's sitting on the floor, who picks it up? It's the person who it bothers more."

It's the same in speaking money, he said. "Someone takes the lead role and someone takes the back seat. The person who takes over is the one who will be more bothered if their goals aren't reached."

Argue Box

Ali		Christine
5' 10"	**Height**	6' 0" (in heels)
working on it	**Weight**	nobody's business
safari	**Ideal Vacation**	family farm with the kids
motorcycle	**Vehicle**	minivan
"Leave this place better than I found it."	**Motto**	"We have two ears and one mouth. Listen twice as much as you speak."
Everyone who struggles against tough odds.	**Hero**	Thomas Edison
aggressive	**Investor Style**	cautious

Obviously we are different. But our differences don't make us incompatible.

We're also (thankfully) not married to each other. Each of us has a real-life spouse with whom we negotiate the budgetary, investment, and other financial responsibilities that every family has. But you'd be surprised at how many couples have widely divergent perspectives on financial matters, and how difficult it is for them to achieve a satisfactory compromise.

It's often said, fights about money are the number one cause of divorce in this country. And, in a recent poll conducted by the National Foundation for Credit Counseling (NFCC), more than a quarter of all respondents said that their financial situation was the leading cause of stress in their marriages.

Gail Cunningham, spokesperson for the NFCC, wasn't surprised to hear it.

"Financial concerns stay with you 24 hours per day, seven days a week," she said. "They are there when you wake up and when you go to sleep, at work, and at home."

Today, with the economy still in turmoil, and with unemployment and underemployment high, financial stresses are likely to be particularly troubling for families.

The recent 18-month recession was declared officially over way back in June of 2009. But many consumers still feel the pressures.

In fact, a recent Gallup survey revealed that more than half of Americans believe the U.S. economy is in a recession—or even a depression—in spite of what the economists tell us.

But it's not only the unemployed who feel the stress. Those people who are fortunate enough to be employed are likely working long hours, taking on extra responsibilities and accepting pay freezes and declining benefits, any of which could add to their level of discomfort.

These stresses affect us in our roles as parents, spouses, and significant others. Concerns related to the basics of life, things such as paying the rent or mortgage, putting food on the table and keeping the lights on can wear on people and put significant strain on their home life, something the children cannot ignore.

To get through the difficult times, (cue that old cliché) communication is key. Although we disagree about many of the specifics of handling money, we recognize how important it is to communicate with your partner, to be honest about the situation, about your feelings, and to discuss the issues as unemotionally and rationally as possible.

Of course, if you're a single individual living by yourself, you have the luxury of doing things your way without any interference from others. If you have a spouse, though, or you live with a

 How to Speak Money—*Talking Points*

Christine says
Many couples make a major mistake: They think financial planning is saving for the dining room furniture or getting ahead of the Disney cruise for next year. Those are the kinds of financial plans that should be tangential to the overall picture.

Most people only think of things that matter to them right now, and that's what they're saving for and working toward. There's a whole world out there that needs to be addressed first, before they get to that. People need to take a more holistic view.

If you have the big picture in mind, if you know what you want your money to do for you and you're working toward that goal, then saving for the vacations and all these other things becomes easier.

significant other, then you must be able to talk about finances and develop a plan that pleases you both. You must be able to do three things: verbalize, strategize, and—yes—compromise.

Verbalize: You have to be able to discuss your feelings, to articulate the concerns you have and to be very specific about them. If you keep your eyes on the future and your significant other is too focused on the here and now, you must find a way to communicate that you're not comfortable with his course of action.

That's easier said than done, of course. In fact, couples therapists have many techniques for helping people overcome the difficulty in initiating this awkward but crucial first step. There are few areas of marriage more contentious and almost none more important.

Our friend Jeff Gardere, often called "America's psychologist," gets close-up views of interpersonal dramas regularly. As "Dr. Jeff," he's a well-known figure on television programs and a sought-after speaker on family topics. Couples bring their financial issues to his office with alarming frequency.

"The most important thing," he said, "is to realize that there is a problem and that one person can't fix it alone. A couple has to work together in solving whatever the problem is."

Often, he noted, the issues are deeper than they may seem at first. "It's not just about someone being weak or being addicted to the pleasure of shopping—there are issues behind those behaviors. It's complex."

Today's economy doesn't help. "Almost every couple I work with and almost every single person I know," said Dr. Jeff, "stresses out about money—making enough money, paying their bills, worrying about whether they can pay their mortgages, what's going to happen in the future, whether they can retire. So it's a major, major issue."

Many financial worries are logical. They're not psychological symptoms of deeper emotional problems. Dr. Jeff believes that it's completely appropriate to have financial concerns in today's difficult climate. So when do money worries cross the line into problems that require a therapist's assistance?

Dr Jeff again: "It's when your anxieties or worries about money keep you from fulfilling your responsibilities—whether it's being a father, a mother, a worker, or whatever your job is in life. If you're unable to work or you're compromised at work, that's when professional help is appropriate. If, for example, you're acting out with alcohol, drugs, or affairs; if you're keeping secrets; if you become a shopaholic; if you're at each other's throats—that is the major distinction.

"It's normal for all us to have worries about money," he said. "It's when those things interfere with your functioning that I, as a professional, would be concerned."

Ultimately, he said, "The couple must find happiness and stability in their relationship, and that will help solve the other issues that are going on."

Strategize: maybe you weren't born speaking the same language. Fine. Once you recognize and bring up the problem, you're going to have to figure out a way to work together and solve it. If your husband's desire to save every last penny means that you never get to go out to dinner, you may suggest having a date night every other week or so. If it's a question of whether you can afford that new furniture, new car, or new school, discuss it rationally, understanding that each of you may view money very differently.

If you look at the issues that divide you, and you consider them from every perspective, the chances are very good that answers will suggest themselves. The more you can open up the lines of communication, the greater the likelihood of successful resolution. It may not be easy, but it almost certainly will be possible. When you realize that some of the most explosive geopolitical problems of the century have been defused over a conference table, you can see that your interpersonal financial troubles can probably be resolved in the same way.

Compromise: Look for areas of agreement, not the places you always fight. Chances are you both understand what's at stake and why you need to make some changes. Seek to meet one another halfway. Look to make your money go further. Again, consider the bigger picture. You're seeking to mend, or at least improve, what is probably the most important relationship in your life. Don't try to win the battle at the expense of losing the war.

Ali and his wife used to fight about restaurants on vacation. She liked fancy; he liked simple. The in-between restaurants on which they invariably settled pleased neither of them. So they divided the nights: She got half and he got half. Now, when Ali sits in a three-star restaurant that his wife has chosen and he dines on an exquisitely prepared multicourse meal, he relaxes. And the next evening, when Lori's standing on a corner as her husband hands her some curious-looking street food he's just purchased from a vendor with a wheeled cart, she goes along with the adventure.

Neither has a high degree of investment in the other's decision, so much less is at stake for each of them. They've managed to let go, and that's often the first step to coming out ahead.

How to Speak Money's Words to the Wise

1. Openness (*oh'•p'n•ness*): Money is a complicated subject for each of us. It's fraught with baggage on many levels. So recognize that others may have their own ways of speaking money that are as valid as your own, even if different.
2. Honesty (*on'•ess•tee*): In almost any relationship, money can be a minefield. But couples should discuss the subject honestly with one another—they need to share their goals, their attitudes toward money and their spending habits. Ideally, they should do so before marriage.
3. Love (*luv*): Be nice to your significant other when you're fighting about money. Try our three *Speaking Money* steps to conflict resolution: (1) *verbalize* (bring up the issue), (2) *strategize* (discuss the things each of you could do to remedy the situation) and (3) *compromise* (develop a plan in which each of you gives a little). Remember, your goal is to solve the problem, not win an argument.

CHAPTER 3

Gendernomics

To say that men and women are different is only to state the obvious. The Mars and Venus analogies scarcely scratch the surface of the many subtle and important distinctions between the genders. We've all made our own observations and the list is endless. But our clichés can't capture the nuances of the complex human condition.

Today there are more women graduating from college than men. The most recent Census data (for October 2009) shows a record 56 percent of college students are women. Grad schools and professional programs are chock-full of smart, aggressive young women who are remaking our definitions of *motherhood, job,* and *company.* They grew up in two-income households. They watched their parents share household duties. Nothing is foreign to them and everything is up for grabs.

But the sexes, for now, still hew to gender roles in the workplace. Consider this anecdote related by Nell Merlino, the founder of Take Your Daughter to Work Day. A female trainer of flight students told her this story. Eighty percent of pilots are men. "With male pilots, you have to bring their skill level up to their confidence level. With female pilots, almost without exception, you have to bring their confidence level up to their skill level."

Women are slowly beginning to take more risks in the marketplace, and you can clearly see that in entrepreneurship. More and more, they're grabbing the reins and opening their own businesses.

As of this writing, in fact, there are an estimated 8.1 million women-owned businesses in the United States, generating nearly $1.3 trillion in revenues and employing almost 7.7 million people.

Those numbers are particularly striking when you consider that between 1997 and 2011, when the number of U.S. businesses increased by 34 percent, the number of women-owned firms increased by 50 percent—a rate one-and-a-half times the national average.

The easiest way for your children to learn about money is for you not to have any.
                    —*Katharine Whitehorn, British journalist*

Women are taking these risks and starting businesses because they now have the education, the funding, and the confidence to make it happen on their own. Sometimes it's because they're fed up with the corporate ladder. Some want more flexibility: They've taken the off-ramp to have a child or care for a parent; now they want to work again, but they want to make the rules for themselves. Still others see a bright idea and want to follow it through on their own and not give it to the boss. Whatever the reason, we think it is clear that a potential huge driver for employment growth over the coming decades will be women starting businesses.

But despite the fact that women-owned firms account for 29 percent of all enterprises, they employ only 6 percent of the country's workforce and contribute just under 4 percent of business revenues. What does this mean?

It means that, for all their success in *starting* businesses, women have a tougher time *growing* their businesses. They're more apt to try to do it all themselves, beginning in their kitchens or living rooms and taking on very few employees. According to Merlino, a forceful advocate for women-owned businesses, they're not thinking big enough.

"Seventy percent of all woman business owners are at $50,000 or less in annual revenue," she tells us.

"You can't make much more than $250,000 by yourself," Merlino explains. "You need to surround yourself with other people. It can be vendors or contractors, it can be employees, it can be advisors, but a lot of women think that for a business to be *theirs*, they have to do everything themselves.

"But the fact is," she says, "you need to define that special thing that *you* do, and then find people who are better with the other parts—the finances, the marketing, or whatever it is.

"What I try to teach women is that starting a business and multi-tasking for more than two or three months is a mistake. It certainly will impede your growth if you think it all has to come from *your* head."

Perhaps women are beginning to take Nell's advice. Women-owned firms are making strides in all industries. Check out these statistics from The American Express OPEN State of Women-Owned Businesses report in March 2011. While the fastest growth in the number of women-owned firms over the past eight years has been in education services (up 54 percent), big gains have also occurred in less traditionally feminine fields, such as administrative and waste services (up 47 percent), and construction (up 41 percent). And in two traditionally male industries—construction and mining—the growth in the number of firms, employment, and revenues has actually outpaced that of the industry as a whole.

But if you're a woman and you're thinking of starting your own business, you might want to know where others have staked their claims. The industries with the highest concentration of women-owned firms are health care and social assistance (52 percent of firms in this sector are women-owned, compared to a 29 percent share overall); educational services (46 percent); personal care services, such as beauty salons and pet-sitting, dry cleaners, and automobile repair (41 percent); and administration and waste services (including employment and travel agencies, janitorial and landscaping services, and convention organizers) (37 percent).

Conversely, the industries with the lowest concentration of women-owned firms include construction (yes, as we've previously noted, women are gaining rapidly in this field, but women-owned companies still represent only 8 percent of the total), and finance and insurance (20 percent). In all other industries, women-owned businesses are close to the 29 percent share they represent across all industries.

Shifting Roles

For generations the division of labor was clear-cut. Fathers were breadwinners, mothers were chiefly in charge of the children, and if anyone had to leave work to take Junior to a doctor's appointment or attend a parent-teacher conference, it wasn't likely to be Dad.

Times change. A nationwide survey in May 2011 found that more than half (56 percent) of employed fathers say they frequently take time off for child-related tasks—markedly more than the 40 percent of mothers who report doing likewise.

Employers haven't quite caught on yet, it seems. About two-thirds (68 percent) of dads with jobs say they've experienced "negativity or problems" with bosses over conflicts between work and children. Of those, 57 percent say this has happened "multiple times."

"The American workforce is different than it was even five years ago," observes Dean Debnam, CEO of Workplace Options, an employee-training consultancy based in Raleigh, North Carolina, which conducted the poll.

For one thing, he notes, the Census Bureau counts 2.3 million U.S. households in which fathers are raising kids alone. Added to the majority of families in which both parents work full-time, "the pressure for fathers to succeed both as professionals and as parents is greater than ever."

Nor is this shift confined to the United States. A global study on men and work/life balance, co-sponsored by Workplace Options and WFD Consulting, found that "finding time to spend with family" was the top concern voiced by fathers in almost every developed nation.

As dads and moms know firsthand—and most employers are beginning to accept—kids' needs are not always predictable in advance. Increasingly, fathers are juggling their family and their job in ways that their own fathers rarely faced. Being a parent "doesn't happen on a set schedule," observes Debnam, adding that combining hands-on fatherhood with a career "takes creativity."

Hear, hear!

Are You Sure We're Talking about the Same Thing?

If we needed more evidence that men and women view money differently, consider their reactions to the recession. A recent survey sponsored by PNC Wealth Management, called "Love and Money," found that men and women are on different pages—if not different planets—regarding the recession's impact on their financial planning:

More women than men express worry about:

- The recession (69 percent of women versus 54 percent of men).
- Inflation (51 percent versus 44 percent).

- Money to support lifestyle (46 percent versus 40 percent).
- Declining real estate values (45 percent versus 35 percent).
- Not being able to support lifestyle in retirement (45 percent versus 34 percent).

From these responses, it would seem that either men are picnicking on the train tracks, oblivious to the oncoming locomotive or that the surveyed women are a bunch of nervous Nellies, fluttering their hands, saying "Oh, my stars!" and looking for the smelling salts.

But even beyond the strictly recession-related issues, the differences between the genders read like the premise for a sitcom—or a beer commercial. Consider these findings:

- Four in 10 men (40 percent) describe themselves as high- or moderate-risk investors. Three in four women (75 percent), by contrast, describe themselves as balanced or conservative investors.
- The majority of men perceive themselves as driving the financial decisions, whereas women say decisions are made jointly. Seventy-three percent of women say they share responsibility for financial decisions; but 53 percent of men claim that financial decision making is mostly their department.

Clearly, both sides can't be right in this case. What accounts for the misperception by one side or the other? Are the men really much more in charge? Are the women down-to-earth and the men blowhards? Are the guys just playing the macho card? Do the women overvalue their contributions? That may be unlikely, since we know that women generally *under*value their worth and competence.

How to Speak Money—*Talking Points*

Ali says
It may be that men make financial decisions without realizing that they've already internalized their wives' points of view. In other words, they've mentally limited their decisions to those their spouses will approve. When the husband says he buys the car, and then he goes out and chooses a very practical minivan in a wife-friendly color, who's really making the decision?

Why Do Smart People Buy Stupid Things?

We'd like to think that we're all rational creatures, able to weigh the pros and cons of a given situation and use our heads to determine the most appropriate course of action. We'd like to think that, but deep down we know it's not true. We're all susceptible to making financial decisions based on emotion rather than reason. These emotional decisions rarely work out and they often leave us feeling bad about what we've done.

But we've all done it anyway. Splurged on something we shouldn't have with money we couldn't afford to spend, bought a stock high and then sold it low. So, why can't we control ourselves?

Well, can you say *neuroeconomics*? It's a branch of science that explores, among other things, why smart people make foolish choices with their money. It's a fascinating field of study.

Using the tools we have today, such as functional MRIs, hormone and genetic sampling, eye tracking, and gaming simulations, neuroeconomics allows us to examine, physiologically, how the human brain evaluates risk and reward over time, which is what investing is all about.

It was our friend, the financial journalist and author, Jason Zweig, who first turned us on to this exciting research. We recently spoke with scientists in this new field. Their neuroeconomic research is shedding light on the tug of war between the physiology and psychology inside our brains. When it comes to money and financial behavior, it turns out that we're all still evolving. And sometimes, what we think we're buying isn't even what we're really after.

Scott Huettel, director of the Center for Neuroeconomic Studies at Duke University, points out that "People don't buy a lottery ticket just because they have a chance of winning. They'll buy a lottery ticket because, over the next couple of days, it allows them to fantasize about what they would do if they won the lottery. In that sense they're paying for the fantasy experience, rather than for the chance at the lottery itself."

Similarly, both men and women can be seduced by the desire to win, especially when the odds of winning are high. But good odds can blind us to big risks. Doug Hirschhorn, an investment psychology advisor who works with traders at top financial institutions, has seen it happen time and again.

"Let's say you had a 95 percent chance to win a game," he said. "Would you play that game?"

"Most people would. But what if every time you win, I give you a dollar, and every time you lose, you give me a thousand dollars?"

Hirschhorn's point is that we can get so caught up in desire to win, based on favorable percentages, that we don't see the huge risks we may be facing. Our brains push us to go for the win, not to soberly evaluate the pros and cons of the given situation. Any casino floor manager can point to hundreds of examples of this trait every night.

Interestingly, with the medical technology available to us today, we can see real-time imagery of the brain's activity. We can see elevated blood flow when people process the gambles in the test situations created for them. We can see interactions of hormones, cortisol, and testosterone in response to risk and reward evaluations. The entire body is involved. It's the modern day version of fight or flight. We sense danger and the opportunity for victory. It's tremendously exciting.

But even as we learn more about our physiological reactions on a molecular level, we still have to deal with ourselves as large, occasionally clumsy creatures seeking to secure food, shelter, clothing, love, status, and all the other components of a happy life.

Despite what we've learned about neuroeconomics, it doesn't make it any easier for Christine to part with a hard-earned dollar or for Ali to keep it in his pocket. But we're certainly more aware of why we are the way we are.

Women and Investing

Compared to men, women live longer, earn less, and take more breaks from the workplace to care for children and elderly parents. And though studies show that women tend to save a slightly higher percentage of their paychecks then men, they ultimately end up with smaller balances because of their lower earnings.

That could mean that women need specially tailored financial advice.

Women who are suddenly single—divorcees and widows, for example—often need help. And singles, in general, may have special needs, like disability insurance, because they don't have a spouse's paycheck to fall back on (though you can make the same case for single men). Financial advisors also say many women need to be prodded to evaluate whether they're being paid what they're worth.

But also consider the changing demographics as reflected in Census data. Men and women are marrying later, and a record low percentage of adults are married today. That means both genders are increasingly going it alone, relying solely on their own financial planning and earnings. It's why the vast majority of financial advice is applicable to both genders.

That's not to say women couldn't use some more confidence in financial matters. For some reason, men seem more adept at faking the accent, if you will, when they speak money. But women don't.

One of our *American Morning* producers exemplifies this. Karrah is a total wonk for politics and public policy. But money? That's another story.

"If it's politics, I speak it," she says. "I don't need briefing books or cheat sheets—I am fluent in that conversation. But talking money is like asking me to speak Chinese. I don't get it. I'm not wired for it. I don't know if it is the words or the vocabulary or the concepts. It's just not an easy language."

Karrah is financially responsible in most ways: She contributes the maximum to her 401(k) and she makes sure she spends less than she earns. After that, though, she looks away completely. Like many women, she both fears losing what she has built and she's terrified by the responsibility of making it grow.

"Maybe it's because personally I am afraid of not having money, and that fear makes the whole language incomprehensible," she said.

People like Karrah—smart and resourceful in every other way—can be undone by their lack of fluency. Because they don't speak this language, they are less likely to be aggressive when asking for a raise. They're less likely to rebalance their portfolios periodically (on the plus side, they're also less likely to panic when the market swoons, because they don't mess with their contribution percentages) and they're also less likely to take a risk that could be profitable down the road.

Karrah asked a question about the language of money—"Which words are most important to learn? Because there's no way can I string a full sentence together."

Our answer is that the most important words are: *financial goals, risk tolerance,* and *discipline.* Everything else fits within those categories.

Translation: What do you need your money to do for you? How much uncertainty can you bear? And discipline? Well, anyone who has ever quit smoking or gone on a diet knows exactly what that word means.

Ironically, the more women accomplish and achieve in the workplace, the less time they have to spend on things like managing their money. And studies show that women don't find money and investing as interesting as men.

According to a 2007 study on gender differences by Tahira Hira of Iowa State University and Cäzilia Loibl of Ohio State University, women are still less likely to be socialized in financial matters, and they are more likely than men to find investment decisions stressful, difficult, and time consuming. The study also found that it often takes a life event, like getting married, to prompt women to save and invest, whereas men were more likely to start investing gradually.

But while women may be less likely to enjoy investing, studies show that they may inherently be better investors than men. Females are less prone to risky behavior, for instance, and, unlike their confident male counterparts, they're more likely to 'fess up to their own ignorance.

We're reminded of a special CNN series called *The Turnaround*. In interviewing countless small business owners to help them turnaround their business, a simple truth emerged. Men were more likely to say, "I don't need your help. I've got it under control." Women were more likely to say, "I *know* I don't know."

Gendernomics in the Workplace

Women have been heading to the office for two full generations now and women do the same jobs as men do—in sales, marketing, finance, planning, and every other area of the corporate world.

But still, despite this progress, women earn less than men for doing the same work. Lee Miller, who with his daughter, Jessica Miller wrote *A Woman's Guide to Successful Negotiating*, believes that a reluctance to haggle holds too many women back.

"Women tend to ask for less," says Miller, who teaches courses on negotiation at Columbia Business School, "And the corollary to that is that you're going to get less."

Consider this: Lee says a $5,000 raise at age 22 is equal to about a half million dollars in salary and benefits over the course of a lifetime.

Although women now earn, on average, 20 percent less than men in the same jobs, Miller says women who improve their negotiating can eat into that difference. He points to recent U.S. Census data showing that single women aged 22 to 30 in major metropolitan areas now earn 8 percent more than their male peers.

Lee calls his daughter—a commercial real estate adviser—the best negotiator around. It takes awareness and an understanding

How to Speak Money—*Talking Points*

Christine says

My incredibly business savvy sister-in-law Kathleen once gave me some negotiating advice that I have passed along eagerly to other women who want to be better negotiators when it comes time for a raise or a promotion.

She told me, "Never give the first number, or you'll be starting too low. Make them give a number first, and then ask for more and always end with a three." Why a three, I asked? "Because when you say it, you finish with a smile on your face!" Bottom line, ask for what you are worth. With a smile.

that you need to make sure that you are getting the best for yourself and are reading the environment around you to make it happen.

"Sixty percent of negotiating is gender neutral. The other 40 percent is different for men and women. It may be different in some of the ways people perceive you. Women bring certain advantages and certain disadvantages to the table."

He talks of the "empathy trap" that women can fall into. The perception can be that women are collaborative and accommodative in the workplace. The key is to be empathetic for other people's needs without giving up what *you* need, Lee says. And then there is that confidence thing again, like the women airline pilots in training who need to get their confidence level up to their skills level.

"Women think, 'Oh gee I'm not good at this, I'm not a negotiator, guys are better at this.' They should not be thinking that. It's something that can be learned," Lee says. "It's like driving. You have to learn it, practice it, and then you can be good at it or better than men."

And here's a funny little twist: Lee says women don't negotiate for themselves very well, even if they're good at negotiating for their companies! In fact, he recounts the tale of the marketing executive who agonized over how to present her bosses with her demands for a better pay package, salary, benefits, and position. She had never in her successful career negotiated on her own behalf—she had always taken whatever was offered to her. Finally, after consulting with a friend, she went for it—and got it.

"When it was all over," Lee says, "She was basically told by (the person) who she was negotiating with that they were impressed with her negotiating and they would have actually been concerned if she hadn't negotiated."

Not negotiating for yourself sets expectations low.

Of course, sometimes it doesn't work. Consider Jana, a successful New York City attorney who twice left a firm so she could move higher somewhere else. When she bumps up against the glass ceiling, she just finds a taller building to work in. Lee sees this often, but cautions jumping ship demands negotiating skills, too.

"Women have more responsibilities at home than men, (so moving jobs) can hurt you if you don't negotiate how to do that balance," Lee says.

There's a phrase we've encountered a lot in our reporting of women and men and their earnings and career paths—*sponsorship*. It's when a woman has a powerful ally higher up in the workplace who is actively *sponsoring* her career advancement. Think of it as a mentor on steroids.

A recent study by Catalyst found that when women lobby for themselves in the workplace, they can be perceived as aggressive or pushy. The study, called Sponsoring Women to Success, found that women can be penalized for exhibiting self-promoting behavior considered acceptable in men but unappealing in women. "Because good sponsors recognize and reward talented employees by speaking up on their behalf, sponsorship can help high-performing female employees subvert this double bind," the study found.

Lee agrees with much of the report, but says at a certain level in their career women need to be better negotiators, sponsor or no.

"If you're gonna play in that league, you have to be willing and able to negotiate for yourself," he says.

So how? Here's Lee's language lesson on "How to Speak Money: Negotiating."

Learn it. Everyone, Lee says, can do it. Men tend to do it earlier in life, but women can do it too.

Don't be afraid. "They tend to be uncomfortable with negotiating for themselves. At least as you move up the corporate ladder, if you're not negotiating for yourself, no one else will. You will be at a severe disadvantage—for compensation and in terms of success compared to your male peers in terms of getting promoted." You can't afford to be afraid.

Negotiate differently. Recognize that men and women can negotiate differently and that is okay. You don't have to be more aggressive or challenging to your boss. Use a firm, quiet, confident tone. State your position quietly, firmly, and do not back off from it, Lee says. "Men tend to trust that when a woman takes a position and stays with it and with a firm, quiet, confident tone, that she means it, and therefore accept it and move on to something else."

We would add that it helps to ask friends and confidantes in the workplace for advice and support. Women should seek out advice from male counterparts and vice versa (as we do!). Men tend to negotiate more often and for more things than their female counterparts probably ever imagined.

Whether it gives you a thrill or makes you sick to your stomach, a successful negotiation is critical for your investment into your career. Of this we are certain.

How to Speak Money's Words to the Wise

1. Confidence (*kon'•fi•dense*): Research appears to support the anecdotally accepted contention that men, for whatever reason, are innately more confident than women in negotiations of all sorts. Women need to recognize this discrepancy and to push through the barriers that keep them from asking for salaries, benefits, and company resources commensurate with their value.
2. Postbiological (*poest•bye•uh•lah'•jik'l*): The differences between men and women have become progressively less important in the workplace, as skills replace strength in the hierarchy of desirable characteristics. But while women are well represented in all phases of public life, from courtrooms to corporations, they still earn, on average, only 77 cents for every dollar earned by a man.
3. Perception (*pur•sep'•shun*): Today's workers are different from those in the past. They want flexibility; they reject the rigidity of a gray workplace. They'd rather meet by Skype than sit in a sterile conference room with a bunch of people in suits. They want the ability to work from home. They want to integrate work into their lives rather than think of it as something distinct. Successful corporations are able to see these differences and respond to them.

CHAPTER 4

Speaking Money around the World

Is there anyone left on Earth who hasn't heard the term *globalization*? We doubt it. It's the umbrella word people use to describe the many trends reshaping the way business is done throughout the world. It refers to the internationalization of trade and the competition among countries for resources, workers, wealth, and jobs. It covers the increasingly fluid movement of goods and services around the planet. It's the name given to the economic imperatives that compel businesses to seek the most favorable climates for production and the most promising environments for sales. And it's the one-word explanation we hear most often every time an American job is shipped overseas or outsourced or just plain eliminated.

What globalization really describes is a world in which more people and more nations have access to the benefits of modernization. This change is both rapid and dramatic. It can take a country from the pre–industrial age to the Internet in a single bound. As recently as 1954, for example, there was a small tribe in the Himalayas that had never seen a wheel. When they saw their first one, it came attached to a DC-3 twin-engine cargo plane. Granted, that's an extreme case, but it illustrates the way today's technology can leap over intermediate steps and catapult a people into the thick of the modern era.

Today, in Asia and Africa, villages that still lack basic sanitation have satellite TVs and cell phones. The wiring of the world has outpaced more traditional infrastructure projects by a wide margin.

Why? Because it's easier, faster, and less expensive to build a network of cell towers than it is to build a network of highways. It's easier to deliver the Internet than it is to deliver clean drinking water.

So the growth of cheap, fast communications—and the attendant dissemination of information to a global audience—have consequences both good and bad. It's enabled farmers in India to conceive of a future for their children that doesn't include back-breaking labor and early death. It's made it possible for factories in Malaysia to serve as the seamstresses of haute couture fashion. And without cell phones and untraceable prepaid phone cards, terrorists would have a much tougher time relaying their plans to one another.

People sometimes forget that business is not a social program. In our capitalist economic system, the prime purpose of business is to earn a profit. In this universe, labor and management are in a relationship that is inherently adversarial. Management—those responsible for the bottom line—will always seek to produce goods and services at the lowest cost and to sell at the highest price that the market will bear. Labor, on the other hand, will always seek to obtain the highest wages, the most comprehensive package of benefits and the best working conditions.

A Brief History

A hundred years ago, the balance of power was heavily weighted in favor of management. To address this unfairness—and to head off violent social unrest—the government permitted unions to be organized so that rank-and-file workers could bargain, collectively, for what they saw as their rights. For the last two-thirds of the twentieth century, the system worked very well.

In industries as diverse as automobile manufacturing, steel production, transportation, and utilities, blue-collar workers—those who did the demanding, uncomfortable, and often dirty jobs required in a country on the move—saw their living conditions rise to standards unimaginable in the rest of the world. A man who carried a lunch pail to work five days a week (not six, as in other countries, but five), could afford to own a home and a car (or two), could take two weeks of paid vacation, could have his family's medical bills paid by his employer and could retire after 20 years of work at half-pay. All this with a high school education. Or less.

The reason companies could afford to treat workers so generously was because there wasn't much competition. Just about everything was made here in America. Most countries didn't have big factories. Some didn't even have *roads*. Others had no infrastructure at all, really. If they had somehow managed to build a factory, they wouldn't have been able to generate enough electricity to run it.

Who was going to challenge us? Europe? How? They went straight from the Great Depression to World War II. The continent was a wasteland and the population had been decimated. They needed whatever energy and resources they had left to defend themselves against the big Russian bear threatening to claw through the Iron Curtain just to the east. And Europe had become semi-socialist anyway, so workers didn't have to work very hard or produce very much so long as the government could keep them employed. The whole idea of personal striving was considered unseemly.

In Asia, it was worse. Yes, we helped rebuild Japan after the war, and by the 1960s the Japanese were turning out millions of transistor radios and giving us Godzilla, Rodan, Mothra, and a host of similar screen giants. But we couldn't really imagine them competing with us where it mattered—in basic industries, major appliances, and sophisticated electronics.

China couldn't get its act together at all, what with Mao advocating a state of perpetual revolution and the Red Guards throwing college professors out of windows. India was tied to its caste system, perhaps the least socially mobile construct ever, a divisive arrangement guaranteeing that untold millions would never have the opportunity to use their brains on behalf of their country.

A bit south and east, Malaysia was just emerging from a long colonial sleep. The people of French Indochina, the region that became Vietnam, Laos, and Cambodia, were engaged in wars of liberation guided by communists. Even if they threw out the French, it wasn't very likely that they'd follow the capitalist economic model.

Korea? First, it was occupied by the Japanese; then the Korean War split the country into North and South; then the South was governed by a series of corrupt dictators and then the military took over. Every time Korea tried democracy the world was treated to images of armed riots. We cared because Korea was a central element in our China containment policy, but the country was poor and backward and seemed destined to remain that way.

So the United States enjoyed a golden monopoly on production. We had the resources, we had the money, and we had the workers. And because our workers were well paid, we also had the monopoly on consumption. Who else but Americans could afford to buy these televisions, dishwashers, cars, and air conditioners?

People overseas, even rich people, had a hard time affording our products. It wasn't just because there wasn't really a labor force or a middle class or a market economy, although those were certainly the main reasons. But in addition, most countries slapped very high tariffs on foreign goods. A TV that cost $300 in Phoenix might cost $900 in Singapore. The United States reciprocated—we, too, used tariffs to protect our industries from cheap offshore competition, should it ever appear.

Climbing Up the Ladder

But something happened. Countries looked at the world around them and decided they wanted what that world had to offer. The generation of revolutionary leaders, men like Mao Zedong and Ho Chi Minh, passed away, allowing a younger, less doctrinaire group to assume control. Their governments became more interested in satisfying the needs of citizens and less interested in promoting rigid ideologies. As Deng Xiaoping famously remarked, "Who cares if the cat is black or white, as long as it catches mice."

Slowly at first, and then more rapidly, things began to change. According to *The CIA World Factbook*, as recently as 1990 the United States accounted for more than one-fourth of the entire world's economic activity: We contributed $5.2 trillion worth of goods and services to a total global output of $20.3 billion. By 2010, the situation was quite different. Although we had nearly tripled the size of our economy—to $14.7 trillion—our share of the global marketplace had fallen to 19 percent. That's because the rest of the world is growing at a faster pace.

The poster child for national transformation is China. A nation of more than a billion people has risen from poverty to prosperity in less than a generation. The pace of growth has been stunning. The world has never seen anything like it. And it has taken place in a society that, while not as repressive as it once was, still lacks many basic freedoms we Americans take for granted.

Technology companies found this out the hard way. Google searched for a new market in China in 2006, but ran afoul of Chinese rules that censored discussion of democracy and human rights.

"Google hoped for a more open China," said Gordon Chang, author of *The Coming Collapse of China,* "but it didn't happen. Censorship got worse during this period and the Chinese government's hacking program got worse, so Google said, 'No more.'" Early in 2011, Google moved its Chinese search engine to Hong Kong.

Yahoo! faced international outrage when it cooperated with Chinese authorities that wanted the identities of people who were using Yahoo to send messages about democracy.

Still, the operating assumption among tech executives (and, frankly, State Department officials) has long been that given time, search engines, social media, and technology will open China, not close it. History will settle that argument.

But for most foreign firms doing business in China—auto companies, grain companies, law firms, manufacturers of electronics and so forth—the dilemmas are more prosaic, having to do with profits rather than protests. Most earnings must stay in the country, for example. Copyright infringements are investigated and prosecuted with decidedly less zeal than are, say, democracy advocates or Falun Gong members. For companies that moved their factories to China, low wages (the original draw for big American corporations) are now rising.

Despite these hurdles, China remains a huge draw for U.S. investment. And because of its rapid growth—and political system seemingly at odds with America's, many Americans cast a wary eye to China's growing clout.

Many people believe that China's rise has come at the expense of the United States. Because while China's lower labor costs allow it to offer products more cheaply than we could, the more we buy those products, the more our middle class jobs disappear.

At the same time, though, China's growth has brought about the development of a middle class there. And that means potential customers for *our* products. In 2010, General Motors sold 2.4 million cars in China: that's 200,000 more than GM sold in the United States. Ford's sales in China rose 40 percent in the same period. In short, U.S. automakers are succeeding in China on a scale unthinkable just a few years ago.

A *How to Speak Money* Riddle

Q: What international crisis did Grandma cause when she dropped Thanks-giving dinner?

A: She caused the downfall of Turkey, the overthrow of Greece, and the breakup of China.

A Fish Story

You can see an example of globalization—and of the power of the Chinese economy—by sitting down to a meal at just about any chain seafood restaurant. Chances are that the fish on your plate spent its entire life swimming around in the open ocean, or in circles in a massive fish farm somewhere. But no matter how many miles it swam when it was alive, it traveled a much longer journey as a product.

Many seafood restaurant fillets come from a fish called Alaska sole. It's a mild, white-fleshed creature, caught in the Bering Sea, frozen on board ship and unloaded in one of the many fishing ports that dot Alaska's coast. From there, though, it doesn't go to a restaurant. Most, if not all, of it goes to China.

The reason is economics. Bill Orr, president of Signature Seafood, told us his catch is cleaned and filleted significantly faster and more cheaply in Chinese workshops than in the United States.

"We sell our fish to companies across the world," he said. "Most of them send the fish to China, where it's processed into fillets or other portions. They have sauces added or have it breaded, then they have it packaged and sent back to Europe, the United States, or South America."

So chances are that the fish you are eating at Cap'n Bill's or Squid Row or any similar restaurant traveled as many as 14,000 miles, depending on where you live. From Alaska or wherever it was caught or farmed, to China to be processed, back to the West Coast ports, then onto trucks and rail cars to destinations in the U.S. interior.

How can that be feasible? Because China's economic miracle of cheap labor and a government-sponsored industrial base has changed everything—even the food on your dinner plate.

The numbers prove it. In 1996, the United States exported $82 million worth of seafood to China. Today, just 15 years later, that number is $597 million. How much of that fish comes back to the United States is impossible to know in this new, globalized world.

The allure of China's market, with its cheap manufacturing base and its one billion potential customers, may be fading, though. As China booms new rules are starting to restrict foreign companies of all kinds. And that has Congress periodically howling for tariffs on goods imported from China, to help correct what it sees as its unfair advantage from China's China-first rules and it's practice of keeping its currency pegged to the U.S. dollar.

"We are going to give the Chinese tough medicine," Senator Chuck Schumer (D-NY) has said.

"We are going to say, 'We're going to impose a penalty on you that will equal the advantage you gain from manipulating your currency,'" he continued.

But are we going to give China tough medicine or just tough talk? The truth is, if we slapped a 30 percent tariff on Chinese goods in an effort to punish the Chinese, it would mostly punish less affluent Americans, who would see dramatic increases in the price of T-shirts for the kids, jeans, consumer electronics, computers, and everything else.

Would Americans be willing to pay more for goods now made in China? What if it meant that more jobs would stay in America, because the tariffs would make it less expensive to produce those same products here? That, in essence, is the debate.

As of now, Bill Orr will keep sending his fish overseas for processing.

"I know it doesn't seem practical to send your product to China and then back to the United States," he said. But apparently it is. "If we did it onshore," he said, "our cost would be about 20 to 25 percent higher than it is now."

And that means you'd pay more too.

Globalization: Good or Bad?

There appear to be two views of globalization. One sees globalization as the killer of American jobs. The other sees globalization as the wave of the future. The first one is partly true. The second is completely right.

Argue Box

Ali says

When looking at how to prepare yourself for work, you need to look at careers that are global in scope. I'm talking about being able to market yourself as a visa employee somewhere else in the world, the same way visa employees come to the United States. Not every person who applies for a visa here is in dire straits. There are Chinese and Indian engineers who are at the top of their game and choose to come here because they'll get the most money, or they like America, or whatever the case is. Why can't we do the same thing in reverse?

Christine says

I don't think it's practical. The advice that you hear sometimes from job placement people is that you should go to China or India to find a job. I just don't think it's practical for the vast majority of middle class American kids to try to get a job in China. In fact, many countries have very strict laws and rules making sure that their citizens get jobs first. Their interest quite frankly is building their own middle class, not giving jobs to ours. Besides, I am not willing just yet to give up on the hope that America is the land of opportunity. What are we saying about ourselves if we say the opportunities are not here any longer?

One can argue that globalization hurts poor countries, making it increasingly difficult for them to afford basic agricultural commodities—wheat, cotton, pork—as a growing worldwide middle class bids up the price for finite resources.

In the decade since China gained entry into the elite club called the World Trade Organization, its exports and imports have surged. America is exporting more to China than ever before, but China is exporting far more to us. That results in a yawning trade gap that highlights, even three years after the financial crisis, the huge structural imbalances remain in the world. Take just one month of official U.S. trade statistics: In June 2011, the U.S. exported $7.7 billion dollars of goods to China. Coming into America's ports in that same month? Almost $34.4 billion in Chinese-made goods.

China's role is felt everywhere. Take housing, for example. Interest rates have been very low, because we've been able to borrow so much money from the Chinese. Depending who you ask, it's either a boon to anyone borrowing money in this country, or it enabled the housing crisis.

And then there is the retail factor. No question the American middle class has been able to buy all kinds of consumer products from China at very, very low prices, helping them feel better and richer in the process.

Argue Box

Ali says

I see a lot of opportunity in the rise of China, but people need to take advantage of it. Take a motel owner in Atlanta who needs to renovate the motel every 10 years. He now understands that the single biggest group of travelers, business or otherwise, is going to come from China. So why not find out what the Chinese like in their rooms? Why not have all your signs and literature in both Chinese and English? Why not get a Chinese website and have Chinese food on your menu?

You know the Chinese are going to go on the Internet, so create a website. Hook up with a travel agent somewhere and start actively courting the Chinese market. You don't have to learn Mandarin, but you could. You've got to hire someone, so why not hire somebody who speaks it already?

Globalization doesn't have to be some international trend that you've got nothing to do with. You can take advantage of it. It's opportunity. And it's here.

Christine says

Yeah, that's great, but you've got manufacturing plants that have been decimated. You've got whole towns that are dead. I believe we've underestimated China's rise, and we've been caught a little off guard by what it's going to mean for America and the middle class. We outsourced factory jobs with the hope that something new, innovative, better paying and service oriented was coming.

But the American family doesn't move that fast. A factory worker doesn't turn into an inventor in ten years. So what are we going to do? Are we going to retrain 13.9 million people to be scientists and mathematicians? What kind of country are we building if the fastest growing occupations are cashiers and retail clerks? (They are.) And when jobs go overseas so companies can save money, will the wealth that companies saved by shipping labor overseas comes back to society as a bill that the U.S. government—and that means the American taxpayer—has to pay for a whole segment of society that can't get a job? These are all troubling questions as yet unanswered in the globalization debate.

Some of our readers are going to blame many of America's ills on a rising China and an American inability to manage that rise. Others are going to say, "No, this is progress. Corporate America is sending its factory floor someplace else because the design and engineering and innovation is here in America." We have found it's more complicated than that.

What Goes Around Comes Around

Ironically, as the rest of the world makes gains, America may increase its manufacturing lead. According to a new analysis by the Boston Consulting Group (BCG), the United States is likely to experience a manufacturing renaissance within the next five years, as the wage gap with China shrinks and certain U.S. states become some of the cheapest locations for manufacturing in the developed world.

With Chinese wages rising at about 17 percent per year and the value of the yuan increasing slightly, the gap between U.S. and Chinese wages is narrowing. Meanwhile, flexible work rules and a host of government incentives are making many states—including Mississippi, South Carolina, and Alabama—increasingly competitive as low-cost bases for supplying the U.S. market.

"All over China, wages are climbing at 15 to 20 percent a year because of the supply-and-demand imbalance for skilled labor," said Harold L. Sirkin, a BCG senior partner. "We expect net labor costs for manufacturing in China and the U.S. to converge by around 2015. As a result of the changing economics, you're going to see a lot more products 'Made in the USA' in the next five years."

Those are optimistic predictions, and it is too soon to call it a trend. After all, American companies have already spent billions of dollars building factories overseas. Once you spend the money to move something, and you move because you've lost your competitive edge at home, you're unlikely to turn around and invest billions of dollars someplace else again. That's why foreign governments are so eager for our companies to come over: because once you're there, you stay.

Of course, if oil prices continue to climb, transporting goods from China and elsewhere in Asia could become prohibitively expensive. Then we're likely to see a greater emphasis on products—from food to manufactured goods—sourced and processed closer to home.

That would certainly help those who have paid the human costs of globalization, like Steve Udden. He's a husband, a father of two daughters, and a trade statistic.

His job as a telecom projects manager in Massachusetts went to China. Classified by the U.S. government as a casualty of foreign trade, the government paid him a stipend and invested in retraining for him. Unemployment benefits and COBRA health insurance helped with his expenses, while he hunts for another full-time job.

"We are keeping it level and steady and holding the line," says Udden, "and right now we are okay."

There is, of course, the financial hardship of being outsourced, but also the sense of personal displacement as well.

"I felt like a baseball player that got traded from a team that he loved playing for and loved the fans. I loved my customers. My co-workers were like second family to me," he said.

To understand what's going on in America, multiply Mr. Udden's story by 2.4 million. That's the number of manufacturing jobs estimated to have been lost to China since 2001.

Who's Zooming Who?

It would be one thing if China simply outcompeted us. If, in the game of commerce, they were winning fair and square. But many people say that this is not the case. It's not just sour grapes, either.

Dan Slane, vice chairman of the U.S.-China Commission, notes that the Chinese government arbitrarily controls the value of its currency. In most foreign exchange markets, by contrast, supply and demand set the value for a given currency. But the Chinese government does not allow its currency to float. One U.S. dollar always buys 6.83 yuan (a *yuan* is the Chinese counterpart to the U.S. dollar).

It's been said that arguing against globalization is like arguing against the laws of gravity.
—*Kofi Annan, former secretary general of the United Nations*

"We believe that the manipulation of their currency gives them about a 40 percent advantage, and it puts our exporters at an enormous disadvantage," says Slane.

By keeping its currency artificially low, the Chinese government keeps export prices down. For example, at the current exchange rate, a product that costs 683 yuan would cost $100 U.S. But if the currency floated to its market value—say, 4.1 yuan to the dollar— then the cost of that same 683-yuan product would be $166 and change. And that might make American goods a smarter, more cost-effective buy.

But pressuring China is tricky. Ten years into its rise, China is our banker and the world's factory floor. It is building its military and buying up the world's natural resources. And it doesn't like the United States telling it what to do.

Nor can we afford to antagonize China when we need its help to contain emerging nuclear threats in North Korea and Iran. So as the temperature rises, the American people wonder: Is China an opportunity or a threat? Most knowledgeable people believe the answer is both.

And what about Mr. Udden? After we aired his story on CNN last year, he got offers for contract work and signed up with a company that kept him busy for several months. That led to other opportunities and interviews and, as of this writing, he feels pretty close to landing another full-time job.

"I'm not a Pollyanna, but I'm a keep-it-moving-forward kind of person," he says.

Does he get angry that his job was outsourced?

"I can't," he says. "It was a business decision by a publicly traded company with obligations to its shareholders." Globalization is what it is, he says, adding, "I am optimistic, focused, and managing through this process."

Globalization is more than just a China story, of course. It is the rise of the BRICs (an acronym for Brazil, Russia, India and China); it is the test of the Eurozone and the common currency in Europe, which is showing strain from cracks in its regional version of globalization; it is the amazing free flow of money and information around the world with a simple keystroke.

There will be new markets to challenge China's factory dominance, and there will be huge challenges for natural resources around the world as these countries build middle classes that will burn more fuel, eat more food, and demand more comforts and resources. In our view, the story of globalization (Marco Polo and the Silk Road nothwithstanding) is only in its earliest chapters.

How to Speak Money's Words to the Wise

1. Globalization (*gloe•buh•luh•zay'•shun*): As Americans, we no longer have exclusive access to the good life. In fact, it's getting a lot more crowded up there, as the entire world competes for finite natural and human resources. The former include energy, food, and clean water. The latter include brains and skills. That's where you can come in. Whether you surf the globalization wave or whether it knocks you under water depends on your education, your natural smarts, and your ability to recognize new opportunities.

2. Prepare (*pruh•pair'*): Study a foreign language, preferably one such as Chinese, Hindi, or Arabic, that's native to a rapidly growing part of the world. Learn a skill that allows you to work anywhere. Be sensitive to opportunities.

3. Adapt (*uh•dapt'*): Be ready to respond to circumstances in ways that are new and innovative. Keep up with changing times. You can't successfully address today's situations with yesterday's strategies.

CHAPTER 5

Speaking Money at Work

Let's talk about the activity that will consume the majority of your waking hours during your income-producing years. Let's talk about the way you're going to earn your living.

We'll survey the changed landscape of American employment and identify promising areas of growth. We'll separate the healthy industries from those that are withering and we'll try to prepare you to take the steps that lead to the career ladders that can help you climb to the position that's right for you.

You might think that American jobs are in crisis. And you'd be right. At the time this chapter was written, nationwide unemployment figures were hovering at about 9 percent. Actually, the reality is even worse, because the 9 percent figure is based on the universe of people who are looking for work and can't find it. It doesn't include the hundreds of thousands, maybe millions, who have given up and stopped looking even though their unemployment benefits have run out.

Right now, 45 percent of the unemployed have been out of a job for six months or longer. The average length of unemployment is 39 weeks—that's nine months. It's painful for everyone, particularly for the elderly. One in four Americans over 50 has spent their entire savings. Too many others, in the richest nation in the world, never had any savings to begin with.

Ben Bernanke, the Chairman of the Federal Reserve, noted that long-term unemployment in this country is the worst it's been since World War II.

"The consequences of that can be very distressing," he said, because when people are out of work for a long time, "their skills tend to atrophy, they lose contacts with the labor market and with the networks that they've built up. It is a very significant concern and it's one of the reasons that the Federal Reserve has been so aggressive."

But he pointed out that the Fed can do only so much to address the issue. Once people become discouraged and stop looking for work, "job training, education, and other types of interventions would probably be more effective than monetary policy," he said.

We're going to talk about job training, retraining, and education. All of these options can lead to careers that are rewarding in both financial and personal ways. They can prepare you to take part in industries that are growing today and that are poised for an even greater increase in the future.

Making a change—in a job, in where you live, in a lifestyle—isn't easy. But one thing that makes America strong and unique is our work ethic, our mobile workforce, and our ability to adapt and grow. And one thing is certain, the more education you have, the more you are buffered from unemployment. The government says the jobless rate for people with a bachelors' degree is roughly half what it is for someone with a high school education.

What's *right* with America is the knowledge that with the right skills and education there is a place for you to succeed to the very top. What's *wrong* with America is the labor market feels like it isn't working for millions. The fact that the very term "99ers" was

How to Speak Money—*Talking Points*

Ali says

I remember desperately wanting to work. I associated work with importance from an early age, so I started with a paper route and then I worked at a local video store. Three dollars an hour I think I got—and I thought I was a captain of industry! I was a dishwasher at a restaurant. I was a valet at a fancy club. I sold clothes all through college.

My mother was a born salesperson. My father was a born businessman. Fortunately, I got a bit from each of them. But they were both better looking.

How to Speak Money—*Talking Points*

Christine says

My first wage was a little over three dollars an hour, too. It was pulling weeds at a nursery, wading through buckets and buckets of saplings in a greenhouse and crying every time a lazy fat garden snake lifted its eyes to look up at me. That was the most terrifying (and short-lived) job, but I worked endless hours as a babysitter, summer nanny, pizza chef, and delivery driver. You have to make a lot of perfect pizzas before you are entrusted on a lucrative pizza run. By the summers when I was 17 and 18, I was working three jobs to save for college—nanny during the day, pizza at night, stocking shelves and selling memberships at the local Sam's Club on the weekends. Except for the snakes, I loved every minute of it.

invented breaks our heart. So-called 99ers are the people who have now exhausted 99 weeks of jobless benefits—first the state benefits we all pay into, then the federal emergency benefits later.

And in the current jobs crisis, we don't want to minimize the dangers. But we also see that opportunities abound.

So, what are the jobs? Where are the jobs? And how can you find one that fits you?

Speak STEM

STEM is an acronym every CEO, recruiter, job trainer, career coach, and college freshman should know. It stands for science, technology, engineering, and math and even a cursory look at the best paid careers with the lowest unemployment rates shows you why.

Decision makers today are fluent in STEM. Governments around the world are scrambling to make sure their students are taught the right skills to get these jobs and dominate these industries. You should be too.

The highest-paid careers are held by people who speak math and science or by people who know how to do business with the STEM-savvy.

Required reading for anyone deciding which career to study for, to switch to, or to invest in is the excellent research from Georgetown University's Center on Education and the Workforce. (Click on the

"What's It Worth?" report for more at www9.georgetown.edu/grad/
gppi/hpi/cew/pdfs/whatsitworthcomplete.pdf.)

Their finding? Different majors have different economic values
and your earning potential varies greatly by your field of study—
from $29,000 for counseling psychology majors to $120,000 for
petroleum engineering. In fact, nine of the top 10 earning careers
are in engineering. The lowest paid professional careers are almost
all liberal arts fields. Table 5.1 shows the edge that STEM fields
have in the economy. The column to the far right shows you how
much the top earners in these professions take home. Impressive.

Engineering isn't for everyone and doesn't have to be.
(Although, to be frank, we're not doing the best job in the public schools to churn out enough kids with these important skills.)
The jobs market is huge and dynamic and is not made up only of
engineers. The most popular major in college today is a business
major. (Median earnings are $58,000 a year with top earners tak-
ing home $85,000, according to Georgetown's analysis.) The high-
est paid liberal arts majors are those who turned an English degree
into a technical writing career. And the fastest growing professional
jobs are in health care, where the pay scale varies widely from six-
figure doctors to $19,000 a year home health care aides. On the
highest end of the pay scale are jobs using technology. Our point is,

Table 5.1   Top 10 Majors with Highest Median Earnings

	Median Earnings $	Top 75th Percentile
Petroleum Engineering	120,000	189,000
Pharmacy Pharmaceutical Sciences and Admin	105,000	120,000
Mathematics and Computer Science	98,000	134,000
Aerospace Engineering	87,000	115,000
Chemical Engineering	86,000	120,000
Electrical Engineering	85,000	110,000
Naval Architecture and Marine Engineering	82,000	120,000
Mechanical Engineering	80,000	105,000
Metallurgical Engineering	80,000	106,000
Mining and Mineral Engineering	80,000	126,000

Source: Georgetown University Center on Education and the Workforce.

you can be fluent in STEM even if you are not a numbers whiz by understanding what this new knowledge-based economy means for the skill set you have. Ali majored in religion and Christine in journalism and French. Enough said.

Dirty Jobs

Eight of the top 10 paying careers are engineering. But not everyone is going to college to be a biomedical engineer. Not everyone should, either.

We're big fans of skilled labor and the so-called dirty jobs.

To us, these jobs are ladders to a great living. Look at the pluses: They can't be outsourced, the government says we are going to need more of them, and you can master them even if you can't design computer circuit boards or wireless applications.

We call them *ladder jobs* because they allow you to climb. You start out at a decent wage and you work hard, but you can grow these jobs into a business in which you hire other people and can be the boss. (Of course, you have to be financially fluent to do so!)

Electricians, plumbers, steamfitters, and similar blue-collar fix-it professionals all enjoy above-median incomes. Those at the top of their game earn well over six figures. (Don't get Christine started about the Sunday afternoon when the plumber and his son snaked out a clogged basement drain and, $1,200 later, were replacing a line to the sewer and fishing a broken snake out of the drain.)

One of the main problems with these professions (and that's what they are—skilled trades) is the public's perception of them. They lack status.

As our economy emphasized white-collar jobs and the definition of a good job changed, plumbers, electricians, machinists, and other skilled workers have seen their professions' image suffer. Working with our hands doesn't have the same cachet as working with our heads. An electrician is every bit as important as an office worker and has the income to prove it.

Mike Rowe, the host of the television program, *Dirty Jobs*, believes we're devaluing honest work.

"We've got this great rift in between blue and white collar," he said. Blue-collar jobs "have come to feel like vocational consolation prizes. We are simply not celebrating their contribution."

America needs to support skilled labor, Rowe tells us, because America's infrastructure needs welders, pavers, electricians, and the like. And Rowe believes there are millions of shovel-ready jobs that could bolster the American economy. He's so passionate about it, he testified before Congress.

It looks like Rowe is correct. According to the Department of Labor, plumbing and steamfitting jobs will rise 16 percent by 2018, while skilled construction jobs grow by 19 percent. It might be difficult to find qualified workers to fill these needs—we have an aging workforce that will retire soon and we don't currently have enough trained individuals to pick up the slack.

"I just know that in the end, there's a list of jobs that are nonnegotiable, absolutely essential," Rowe said.

"Who's keeping the lights on? Who's making indoor plumbing a reality? Who's keeping the roads smooth? Who's keeping the runways well-paved? Those jobs are no less important today than they were 50 years ago. They're just not celebrated in the same way."

According to Rowe, there are jobs waiting for those with the skills to take them. "There are 200,000 jobs right now in manufacturing that are vacant. There are 450,000 jobs in utilities, transportation, and trades right now—they can't fill them. You're talking about half a million well-paying jobs. At the same time, you've got nine percent unemployment."

Closing the skills gap isn't just important for the people who could be hired or for the companies desperate to hire them. "It's important for all of us," said Rowe, "because we all pay the price for bad roads."

Green Jobs

The need to cultivate sustainable sources of energy has led to the growth of *eco* jobs—those that have to do with the environment. We don't mean traditional wildlife occupations like forest ranger, which require a specialized path of study while you're in college and are most often on the state or federal payroll. Instead, we're talking about private sector opportunities in fields such as wind energy.

Wind power has been used for centuries—think Holland and its windmills—but it's a relatively new source of electricity. Here in the United States, it's a fast-rising industry: up 39 percent a year from 2004 to 2009, and it's expected to grow more quickly as the demand for renewable energy increases.

The United States has increased its wind-generated electricity capabilities over 10-fold since 2000. We already produce enough to power almost 10 million homes. Iowa receives approximately 20 percent of its electricity from wind power. The figure is growing nationally: By 2030, it's estimated that 20 percent of the electricity used nationally will be supplied by wind.

It's easy to see why wind power gets the support of politicians and the public alike. Wind is nonpolluting, wind is plentiful, and wind can't be controlled by a group of countries that may not have our interests at heart. As the industry grows, it's creating many more jobs. They aren't just on the wind farm, either. You find them in factories and offices, too, because it takes many different skill sets to build and operate wind turbines.

There are wind power jobs in manufacturing, in construction, and in operation and maintenance. Responsibilities for the production of equipment are divided among numbers of suppliers. From the steel turbine towers to the fiberglass blades to the turbine's nacelle—the rectangular box holding the turbine's brain—many companies have a hand in producing the 8,000 individual parts that make up a turbine.

There are also many jobs in the project development phase, beginning with site selection and continuing through legal and financial issues, community relations and more. And we haven't even discussed the complexity of erecting the turbines themselves, work that generally requires specialized trucking companies to haul large equipment to remote locations and expert construction crews to assemble the components.

How to Speak Money—*Talking Points*

Ali says

You have to think of yourself as a long-term, blue chip stock. And when you're at work, make sure your bosses think of you that way, too. Be something that they need; somebody stable with an honest and consistent return.

Once the turbines are in place and running smoothly, they must be monitored to ensure that they're generating power most efficiently. While much of this work can be done remotely, wind techs perform the routine checks and necessary preventive maintenance on site. They climb up the ladders housed inside the towers and, 300 feet up in the air, they need to diagnose and fix problems quickly, since the energy company loses money every minute the turbine is shut off.

We've used our wind power story to illustrate a basic fact about today's job market: With a little specialized training, you can often leverage your experience and transfer your existing knowledge from one industry to another. Very few of the jobs we've discussed here require skills unique to wind power. The Department of Labor goes out of its way to remind us that, "For most positions, the wind companies hire people with experience in other industries and give them wind-specific training."

That's good news for people who have seen their current jobs suddenly arrive at a dead end. It means that they now have an opportunity to transition into a better future, one with real growth potential.

Women and Work

In the 1950s, women comprised roughly 30 percent of the workforce. Today, according to the most recent numbers for the Department of Labor, it's about half.

But that impressive increase comes with some troubling side effects. In families with two working parents, women continue to shoulder the primary responsibility for child care, and a woman's career often takes a back seat to her husband's.

Look at Linda Reale, who for 20 years built a career at one of the Big Four accounting firms. Despite her professional success, she could never escape the social and biological demands of womanhood.

"I think that women—whether you're married with children, single, no matter what—face challenges," she said. "I know I have my family's demands, my husband's demands and, importantly, I have work demands."

Then Linda's husband was suddenly transferred overseas. And she faced taking the off-ramp.

"I felt overwhelmed with what was I going to do from a professional perspective and a personal perspective," she said.

Fortunately, Linda's employer allows employees to take time off—to raise children or care for aging parents—and come back to their jobs. But although big companies are offering more flexibility than before, many women find they can better balance their lives by working for themselves.

Some women are trying to take the on-ramp back to their old jobs. Many others are trying to make new ones for themselves.

Our friend, Rod Kurtz, is the executive editor of *Huffington Post Small Business.* He uses the term, *mom-preneurs* (like *entrepreneurs*) to describe this phenomenon.

"I think a lot of moms are saying, 'The heck with the rat race. I'm going to get out there and start my own biz.' They often target niches that corporate America is ignoring and we see these businesses grow quite big," he said.

Women's dive into the entrepreneurial pool is becoming more common. The research firm Intuit recently estimated that by the year 2020:

- The gender gap in earnings will narrow.
- Women will graduate college at a higher rate than men— better preparing them to lead in a knowledge economy.
- Women will be a dominant force in the health education and service sectors.

But no question—the challenges of family and work remain. Linda Reale noted, "I was out of work for 18 months. It doesn't sound like a long time, but you completely change your life: from being a working girl, to being a working mom, to being 100 percent at home and focused on other things. In that sense, it's a really long time."

And for all the rosy talk of women's empowerment, a woman still makes only 77 cents to a man's dollar. The reasons for that could fill another book, but we digress.

Getting a Job

Whether you're looking to make a career switch or you're trying to land your first real job, you can't get anywhere until you persuade a potential employer to hire you. You have to distinguish yourself, to stand out from many others who are no doubt competing for that same position, and demonstrate why you are the right fit—the perfect fit—for the job.

In today's market, being pretty good won't be good enough. You have to be special. You are, of course. Really. No one else is exactly like you. No one else has your exact blend of character, skills, talents, and life experiences. The trick is to weave these elements into a compelling narrative that makes it virtually impossible for an employer *not* to hire you.

Bill Taylor, the founder of *Fast Company* magazine and author of the cult business classic, *Mavericks at Work* and the recently released *Practically Radical: Not-So-Crazy Ways to Transform Your Company,* says it's important to think of yourself as a brand. "Know what you stand for," he advises. "Conduct yourself in ways that are memorable. Be the person others look forward to bumping into in the hallway." In other words, seek opportunities to contribute, to lead, and to make yourself known.

While experts have different views on certain aspects of the hiring process, they all agree on one thing: Sending 50 resumes a day to potential employers will not get you a job.

Instead, experts say, making connections, tailoring your message to each potential employer and promising results are the only ways to get hired.

 How to Speak Money—*Talking Points*

Christine says

Whether it is moving for a spouse's job, to have a baby, to raise young kids, or because you have been downsized, it is incredibly important to fill that gap on the resume with professional or volunteer work. Keep up with professional and industry licensing and associations and don't apologize for taking the off-ramp. Be ready at an interview with a smile and an explanation. "Anyone who can handle three kids under the age of seven would know that wrapping up quarterly reports on time is easy by comparison!"

Make Connections

Your personal connections are the only way you are going to get a job. Friends, former co-workers, former customers, clients, and competitors: These are the people who will mention you when a job opening comes up. No one right now wants to take a risk. They are much more likely to hire a known quantity. The trick is, making yourself that known quantity.

We have said it a million times on TV and will say it again here: the most important name on your cover letter is not yours. It is the name of the person you have in common with the recipient of that cover letter. It's up to you to make that connection with the hiring manager. They are not going to come looking for you through a computerized job board and nothing you write is more important than the connection you share.

Social networking has carved out a crucial spot in connection in today's job market, in part because we can keep our connections with people fresh. LinkedIn, Facebook, and Twitter and any smaller industry-specific sites are really helpful for networking.

We're reminded of one of Christine's friends, who was so overwhelmed by the hundreds of resumes he had received for a job he posted that he turned to Facebook. He posted a message that went something like this: "Anyone know smart people who want to work hard and are low-maintenance and can do some great research for one of my projects? If you personally vouch for them, I'll consider it."

He received references for 14 great candidates and hired all of them.

Social media and technology also allow for creative ways to get attention.

One of our sources, financial planner Stacy Francis, hired someone and she didn't even have a job to fill! A young, eager job seeker studied Stacy's company's online profile and videos, and then submitted a video resume in the same style.

"I hired her on the spot. I figured someone this eager and talented could help grow my business and pay for herself in the end," Stacy says.

But it's only part of the story. Most career counselors, coaches, and recruiters say it's the face-to-face connections that really boost a job seeker's chance of getting hired. You can sit on Facebook all day long and never get a job. You can also be undone by sloppy blog postings and tacky pictures in all your social networking. Keep it professional. Finding a job should be your full time job.

Tailor Your Message

Once job seekers connect with a company, then the real work of getting hired begins. Gone are the days of impressing a hiring manager with experience and education. These days it's identifying what results you can deliver that will ultimately get you an offer.

The cover letter should be short (and as we said, contain the name of the person you have in common) and should state what you can bring to the job and the company. Boilerplate language is verboten.

Tig Gilliam, CEO of Adecco, a huge employment placement firm, says you are pitching yourself, not casting about randomly for open positions. Make it pointed, relevant, and—from the point of view of the company hiring—profitable. Remember, companies hire because they have a problem they need to solve. They need to add a worker only when they need to add to their bottom line. And if they seem reticent, offer to work for a specific length of time to prove yourself. It might be just what a recession-weary manager needs to tip him or her toward pulling the trigger and hiring you.

Gilliam says most permanent hiring today started out as part time or contract work, because companies are still very cautious about adding to their permanent headcount.

The experts also recommend being open to the pay, position, location, and schedule of any position that is offered. We prefer paid consulting as an entrée into a company, but some experts recommend volunteering for an organization, even if it may be several steps below a job seeker's previous position, as a great way to ultimately get hired.

Promise Results

Once you are well versed in the company's particular constraints within the current economic climate, identify what you can bring to the table.

Find your recent and most relevant successes and clearly highlight them. What problem did you solve that cut costs? How did you grow your market or identify a niche that made your company more efficient?

How to Speak Money—*Talking Points*

Christine says

The way the world is now, you have to know how to speak money at your job. No one's hiring you because you're nice. They hire you because you can solve a problem that costs them money. If you know how to solve other problems too, you're increasing your value. That's really the way to think about the job market, especially now.

But how can you demonstrate what you can offer if you're just starting out on a career path? First, do your homework. Find out about the company. Visit the website. Try to talk to employees, or to employees in the same industry, to get a sense of the day-to-day, the key challenges, and the work environment. If you find yourself in an interview, don't ask what the company can do for you; tell them what you can do for the company.

No matter what a nice person you are how much of a team player you are, skittish bosses want to know that you have achieved results before and that you can do it again.

In doing your homework on the company or industry you are trying to break into, work hard to translate your former successes into similar scenarios. Oh, and that part we just wrote about being a "team player?" Don't put that phrase on your resume or cover letter. It goes without saying. Skip the clichés and the big fancy words like "facilitate, transition, and effected."

The Long-Term Unemployed

It's no secret that with unemployment hovering at 9 percent, finding a job today is not easy. And the longer you're out of work, the more difficult it becomes. At the time this chapter was written, fully one-third of the unemployed had not found work in at least a year. Their benefits have expired, their skills are atrophying, and their hopes have dimmed. But they still have to support themselves.

For these people, it may be time to consider retraining. While it's difficult to let go of a self-image, redefining oneself is the only way to move forward. There are many rewarding fields in which there are more jobs than there are people to fill them. It's true in health care, in transportation, and in many other industries. So if

How to Speak Money—*Talking Points*

Christine says

I always caution against feeling emotionally abandoned or neglected if you've lost a job. This isn't your wife or husband; this is a job, and at bottom, it's a transaction. How many great employees were cut in the past few years simply because a budget ax fell indiscriminately? Pick yourself up, make finding a job your full time job, and fill the gap on the resume with ANYTHING. Things are slowly picking up.

you've been laid off, and out of work for months, it may be time to move on.

There are a number of careers in medicine. Ultrasound technologists are in demand and well compensated. A nurse anesthesiologist can make as much as an anesthesiologist with a medical degree. Yes, the training is not inexpensive and can take several years, but you don't need a medical degree to pursue the occupation.

Many promising occupations are in fields such as information technology and computer sciences. If you can make apps, you've got opportunity. It's become so prevalent that science camps now teach application making to 17-year-old kids.

But is it worth it? It's one thing if you're a kid, but say you're 40 or so. When you look at the cost of retraining, does it make sense to change careers?

Let's calculate the potential return on investing in your own transformation. We'll look at going from being a factory worker (a declining industry) to being a registered nurse (a growth field).

Consider earnings. Mean annual wages for a registered nurse in 2010 were $67,720. For assemblers and fabricators—factory workers—they were $31,040. Assume you are 40 years old, and plan to work until 65. You have 25 working years as an assembler or fabricator.

It takes a minimum of two years to get an associate's degree in nursing from a community or technical college, or a nursing diploma (although nursing typically requires ongoing education while you work), so you'd have only 23 working years.

Let's assume you earn the mean in either career, and we'll assume a lower-than-average 2 percent annual raise. A quick calculation shows that your remaining lifetime earnings as an assembler or fabricator will be \$1,045,145 over 25 years. As a registered nurse (which affords better advancement opportunities) you'll net \$2,060,169 over 23 years. Almost exactly double. And when you consider that you may be able to invest some of the difference, your final tally could be even greater.

Now let's look at the outlay. Your transformation costs will include the cost of not working for the time it takes to train and two years of tuition at an out-of-state university; 3 percent inflation on that cost over 25 years; and the cost of education financing, if any. The total comes to roughly \$346,573.

So, your gain (\$2,060,169) minus your cost (\$346,573) gives you a net profit of \$1,713,596. Your "Transformation Return on Investment" is a cumulative 494 percent over 23 years.

That's the equivalent of taking the \$346,573 you spent on education, investing it, and earning a return of 10.2 percent per year for 23 years. That would be an unbelievably smooth and successful run in the stock market.

Obviously, changing careers is a major decision with many factors to consider. There's your qualification, aptitude, desire for the new career, family considerations, and confidence that you'll actually get a well-paying job in your new career *soon*. It helps to choose a new career like nursing, accounting, or engineering, for which employment opportunities will be huge.

Again, in this example, the assumptions are easier than they might be for some. Research into cost of training, wages, job growth, and placement rates is key, and those results don't fit neatly into an equation.

You Wanna Start Something?

Another avenue to consider when you find that you're not getting hired: Hire yourself. Start your own company. That's what Glenn Grossman, a stockbroker, did after he was laid off in his mid-50s. When he couldn't find a job he wanted—or one that wanted him—he started Dinosaur Securities. And yes, the pun is intended. Now he's the one who does the hiring, bringing in the best workers regardless of age.

"I wasn't prepared to work for anyone else," he said. I wanted my own thing. I had had a lot of responsibility before, and I still wanted to have that.

He struggled at first, but eventually his team began to get its rhythm. One thing that sets his firm apart is the wide age range of its staff.

"We have people in their 20s, 30s, 40s, 50s, 60s, and 70s," Grossman said. "Hopefully, we'll have a couple of octogenarians soon."

As for those who say older workers can't keep up the pace, Grossman doesn't buy it. "The 70-year-old guys, they come to work early," he said. "They're enthusiastic. They've got as good a work ethic as anybody, and they are excited about new developments in the market."

And at Dinosaur Securities, Grossman can indulge his inner teacher. "One of the things we like best—we older guys—is taking someone in their 20s, just out of school, and teaching them everything. I love teaching."

So out of necessity, Grossman leapt into the unknown and landed on his feet. "I'm thrilled about what we managed to accomplish," he said. Perhaps his experience will encourage others to take the same path.

Not-So-Happy Campers

Despite—or perhaps because of—today's high unemployment rates, many people who do have jobs don't like them.

According to a recent report by Mercer, an outplacement and consulting firm, working conditions in this post-recession economy have become so onerous half of U.S. employees are actively eyeing the exits or have a less-than-favorable opinion of their employers.

Mercer surveyed 2,400 workers in the United States and hundreds more in other countries over the six months ending in May 2011.

Its report said that nearly one in three American workers is seriously considering leaving his job, up from 23 percent six years ago.

The best way to appreciate your job is to imagine yourself without one.

—*Oscar Wilde, Irish writer and poet*

In addition to that, 21 percent said they have a negative view of their employer and have largely checked out of their job, even if they aren't looking for another one, according to the survey.

This level of dissatisfaction among workers is a red flag for employers, who could face higher retention costs and decreased productivity from a burned out workforce, Mindy Fox, a senior partner at Mercer, told our colleagues at CNNMoney.

"The business consequences of this erosion in employee sentiment are significant," she said.

Of course, many unhappy workers don't have a lot of options right now.

While employers have been adding to payrolls in 2011, the pace of hiring has slowed as the economic outlook has darkened. According to government statistics, the economy gained a mere 54,000 jobs that May, a significant decrease from the 232,000 jobs added to payrolls the month before.

Employers drastically reduced head counts during the 2007–2009 recession, which resulted in higher workloads for existing employees. But given the sluggish recovery in the job market, many workers have been reluctant to leave their jobs, even if they are overworked and unhappy.

The Mercer survey suggests that the combination of extra work and stagnant wage growth have taken a toll on employee morale.

More than half of those surveyed were dissatisfied with their base pay, which Mercer says is the most important element of an employment arrangement. The survey also showed low scores for career development and performance management.

According to the survey, the share of employees interested in leaving has increased at all career levels, but younger workers are the most eager to flee.

So if you're an employee and you fit the description given here, it's clear that you're not alone. And bosses beware. It's a good idea to meet with your workers regularly to discuss their concerns. There's a definite link between employee morale and productivity. You might want to take action before your workforce deserts.

How to Speak Money's Words to the Wise

1. Analyze (*a'•nuh•lize*): To be happy in your job, you need to find something you like, something you're good at, and something someone will pay you to do. Look for the point at which those three lines intersect.

2. Blue collar (*blu•ka'•luhr*): We believe that the skilled trades—electrician, plumber, crane operator, computer repair, and similar occupations—offer excellent and lucrative careers. Our so-called blue collar workers, from oil refineries to tugboats, handle the chores that keep America moving forward.

3. Service (*sur'•viss*): The service sector—everything from plumbers and electricians to radiology technicians and home health care workers—remains a robust slice of the economy, with plentiful jobs. Training is often less expensive and less time consuming than you might think.

6

Speaking Money on Campus

Time has changed the way we look at education. A generation ago, a high school diploma was all you needed to land a good job. We had a robust manufacturing sector turning out everything from raw steel to finished cars. There were blue-collar opportunities around the country, and employers desperately looking for willing workers to fill them. Many of these positions were union jobs, guaranteeing rising wages and a slew of benefits such as health care, paid vacations, and pensions. It was a lifetime of comfortable living, and it provided a secure platform from which a family could be pretty sure of passing on an even better future to the next generation.

So what happened? Basically, that kind of existence became too expensive for companies to fund. Globalization (there's that word again) meant that other countries could turn out the same products we were making at just a fraction of the cost. It also meant that foreign firms had an advantage. It wasn't that they were paying less for the materials that went into our cars, TVs, computers, and dishwashers. No, the commodities markets charge the same to everyone. And it wasn't that companies in other countries paid less to advertise and market their goods. After all, 30 seconds of TV airtime costs what it costs, no matter which ad agency is making the buy. Yes, their factories were newer and somewhat more efficient, but that wasn't the answer, either.

The big price advantages that foreign countries had was low labor costs and even lower regulation. An American worker might make $20 an hour to work on an assembly line and grumble about the low pay. An Asian worker might make $20 a *day*—or considerably less—and be extremely grateful for the opportunity to do so. And those workers wouldn't be getting medical, vacation, or retirement benefits, either.

And what about the American consumer? Did we—as purchasers of the many products that constitute modern life—make sure to buy American, because we stood shoulder to shoulder with our fellow citizens? In a word, no. We looked for the best price for value received, the same as anyone would anywhere in the world. That's how Samsung, Sony, Vizio, and LGE kicked RCA, GE, Zenith, and Admiral out of the TV business. That's how Hyundai and Toyota drove General Motors to its knees. The changing economics of commerce in the increasingly competitive global marketplace meant that American manufacturers could no longer afford to compensate their workers at the level those workers had come to expect.

We all know what happened. We're all aware of the loss of American manufacturing jobs and the shrinking power of unions. It was just a few years ago that the government had to bail out General Motors to keep it from falling off the face of the Earth. It turned out to be a good move: The government—which is really us taxpayers—made good money on the deal and GM is, apparently, now on the road to a solid recovery. But let's not forget how controversial it was, and how many people attacked the loan on principle.

Despite the rebirth of General Motors, the sad fact is that the time of steady wage growth for people with only a high school diploma is behind us. And we won't see those days again. The world has moved on; and we must either move with it or be left behind.

High School Then, College Today

Today, postsecondary education is a must for employment at any kind of company that offers a career path for growth. Companies want skilled workers and, more than that, they want dedicated workers. They want people who think enough of themselves to have made the commitment to further education and who have had the discipline to stick it out. No matter how smart or good you are, without that college credential you don't have a chance.

The difference between college and high school is the difference between designing cars and repairing them. It's the difference between fixing computers and fixing lattes. Paint the likely future of a high school graduate and you're not painting a pretty picture.

Sure, there's always the exception, the rare individual who dropped out of school and started a successful office cleaning business, or who founded a clothing company, but chances are that's not you. And even if it could be, wouldn't it make sense to take the easier and more proven path, to start an entrepreneurial career *after* you've gone to college, broadened your horizons, and gotten more experience under your belt?

The fact is that education is the single most important predictor of future earning power. And if you want to speak money, you have to be able to engage it on its own terms. Consider these statistics from the Labor Department in Figure 6.1.

On the left side of the chart, you can see the unemployment rates for 2010, broken down by education level. The jobless rate for a bachelors' degree holder is about half that for someone with just a high school education. The more education, the lower the unemployment rate. On the right of the chart you see the median earnings in 2010 of those same education categories. Median pay was $782 a week in 2010, but anyone with a degree did considerably better. Over the course of a working lifetime, these few hundred dollars a week mean hundreds of thousands of dollars in earnings.

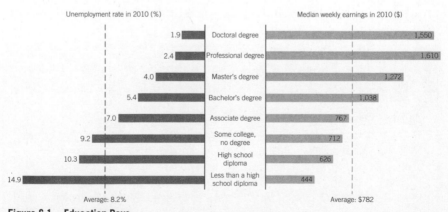

Figure 6.1   Education Pays
Source: Bureau of Labor and Statistics, Current Population Survey.

It's popular to question whether $20,000-plus in student loan debt is "worth it" when the unemployment rate is this high. We think this chart pretty much settles that. The question is not whether you should get a college degree. It's how you pay for it and make sure it is relevant in a fast-changing global world.

A College Degree Never Hurt Anyone

You might be surprised to learn just how much a college degree means in the marketplace. Not just in the obvious occupations, the professions and the corporate world, but in the so-called blue-collar realms as well.

In a recent article, David Leonhardt of the *New York Times* noted that college has big benefits, even in many fields where a degree is not crucial.

He cited research by Anthony Carnevale and Stephen J. Rose of Georgetown that showed that construction workers, police officers, plumbers, retail salespeople, and secretaries, among others, make significantly more with a degree than without one. Why? Education helps people do higher-skilled work, get jobs with better-paying companies or open their own businesses. And beyond money, education seems to make people happier and healthier.

Leonhardt quotes MIT economist David Autor, who has studied the labor market: "Sending more young Americans to college is not a panacea. . . . Not sending them to college would be a disaster."

The most unfortunate part of the case against college is that it encourages children, parents, and schools to aim low. For those families on the fence—often deciding whether a student will be the

 How to Speak Money—*Talking Points*

Christine says
There are amazing opportunities in state schools. If you cannot afford to pay $100,000 for a private school education, a private liberal arts education, you should not be paying for it. You've got to sign up for what you can afford. I think too many kids and their parents are sacrificing too much and taking on too much debt to go to a private, small liberal arts college, where you're going to get the same job in the end as a kid who went to Iowa State.

How to Speak Money—*Talking Points*

Ali says

The single biggest impediment to college is financing. I agree with Christine—there are great opportunities in state schools. And most people can get funding to go. We're competing against many countries that offer free higher education. They've made it a priority. We're not there in America yet; I hope that we get there one day. It's a tough world out there, and Americans have to understand that we need to get in and out of university as effectively and quickly as possible.

first to attend—the skepticism becomes one more reason to stop at high school. Only about 33 percent of young adults get a four-year degree today, while another 10 percent receive a two-year degree.

The biggest argument against college is money. It's true that college costs have increased much faster than the rate of inflation. But it's also true that many colleges are not very expensive, once financial aid is factored in. Average tuition and fees at public four-year colleges were only about $2,000 (though Congress may have cut federal financial aid by the time you read this).

Also, the returns from a degree have soared. Three decades ago, full-time workers with a bachelor's degree made 40 percent more than those with only a high school diploma. Last year, the gap reached 83 percent. College graduates, though hardly immune from the downturn, are also far less likely to be unemployed than nongraduates.

The Hamilton Project, a research group in Washington, has just finished a comparison of college with other investments. It found that college tuition in recent decades has delivered an inflation-adjusted annual return of more than 15 percent. For stocks, the historical return is 7 percent. For real estate, it's less than 1 percent. If you can't see the benefit of higher education, you may need kindergarten again, not college.

The Future Starts in Grade School

We found it surprising—and, frankly, depressing—that in the first Republican presidential debate of 2011, the word *education* was never mentioned. Because, if we want to maintain our place in the world, education needs to be part of the conversation—at home and on the campaign trail.

Education leads to innovation, and innovation leads to jobs. And right now, we need more of both. Believe it or not, we spend twice as much per student as we did a generation ago, yet we're still behind in subjects like math and science.

Do you know what STEM is? It's the future. It's an acronym that stands for **S**cience, **T**echnology, **E**ngineering, and **M**ath. Only 14 percent of all undergraduate students enroll in a STEM subject. Of those, a third will switch out of these fields, and only two in five will graduate with a STEM degree or certificate within six years.

As the president said about STEM, "These are the jobs of the future, the jobs that China and India are cranking out. Those students are hungry because they understand that if they get those skills, they can find a good job. They can create companies; they can create businesses and create wealth. And we're falling behind in the very fields we know are going to be our future."

The truth is, we need quality education to get back to the top. We need our leaders to make it a priority. Of course, it's a complicated and controversial issue. Everyone, from teachers to parents to unions and reformers, has an opinion. But if we're serious about our future, we need to get serious about educating the next generation of Americans. And that means making it part of the political conversation.

So forgive us for standing on a soapbox. But for kids and their parents, education is, rightly, a big, big issue. You can see it in the number of families who move just so they'll be in a good school district. You can see it in the rising cost of private schools—over $40,000 a year in New York City, according to a recent article in the *Wall Street Journal*. That's more than a year at Harvard or Princeton. At those prices, quality education becomes a privilege for the rich, not a right for all Americans. It means that a vast majority of our nation's young minds will never have access to the education that could help propel them into a rewarding future. And that, to us, is just plain wrong.

Education for Life

We know that many different kinds of people will be reading this book. You may be on the verge of college yourself. You may be the parent of a high schooler uncertain of her future. You may be in the workforce wondering if your job is secure, and whether you should go back to school for a degree or for retraining. You may be out of a job and not sure what to do.

Our answer to all these questions: The more education, the better. Get as much as you can afford. BUT—and it's a real but—education does not mean simply spending more time in college. Taking five years to get a four-year degree, a common practice in the grungy 1990s, seems almost decadent in today's climate. By contrast, taking *three* years to get a four-year degree seems noble. It demonstrates a powerful work ethic. (Employers, by the way, love hard-working people.)

Let's look at how the situation has changed. In the old days (and it wasn't all that long ago), people borrowed for college against the rising value of their homes. Today, that's not only foolish, it's impossible. Home values are stuck in the mud and banks aren't lending. Besides, when it comes to education, you shouldn't borrow more than you expect to earn in your first year after graduation. That's a prudent rule endorsed by most every expert we've consulted.

Fortunately, colleges know the score. They're on your side to the extent possible. Many offer accelerated programs that allow students to receive a full education in less time. Almost all universities have summer courses, so that individuals with the commitment to do so can design their own path to graduation on a schedule that meets their needs. And every university provides employment assistance to help students find jobs and work while they're in school.

How Should You Look at College?

Evaluating a college education raises some questions of its own. Should you view college as an opportunity to immerse yourself in the history, literature, science, and cultures of our world and "join the ranks of educated men and women," as a standard line from Harvard's commencement address puts it, or should you view college as a sophisticated trade school? What's the role of a standard liberal arts education in today's more results-oriented world?

These are good questions with no one right answer. We're both liberal arts majors with BA degrees. But neither of us is sure we'd urge others to follow our paths. Too much has changed since our undergraduate years. Today, education for its own sake is a luxury few can afford. That's why we'd stress the practical, career-oriented opportunities the college experience can provide. Still, each of us sees it a little differently.

Argue Box

Christine says

I don't think that there's a margin for error in college education anymore. If you were in Generation X, you could take five years to graduate, you could switch majors three times, you could go save the turtles in Costa Rica if you wanted, because your parents could take a little money out of the house or you could get a student loan. And you were pretty much guaranteed a job, because in Generation X we created 24 million jobs.

Today, in Generation Y, more than eight million jobs have been lost because of the recession, and the class of 2011 is competing with the classes of 2010 and 2009 for jobs. People are trying like the devil just to get into the job market. Times are tougher and the road is harder. You can't have the Gen X mentality for the Gen Y job prospects.

If I could advise young people on a course of study, I would argue for STEM—that means, Science, Technology, Engineering, and Math. Those are the quantitatively based subject areas that will drive growth in the coming century. Those fields will lead developments in computers, in medicine, in materials, and in areas that we haven't even seen yet. And jobs in those disciplines will be in demand around the world.

These are the very fields in which the United States lags. Today's engineers and their STEM counterparts are coming from China, India, and many other countries outside the United States. If we put the same emphasis into designing video games that we put into playing them, we'd be in a much better competitive position. We are the most innovative country in the world, and we can't afford to lose that edge.

The other thing I would say about college is, get in and get out. Do your work, get your diploma and start your life. Ali and I have both argued for three-year degrees. The recently published book *Academically Adrift* found that after two years of college education, the typical college student has learned nothing. Another recent study found students spend more time drinking each week than studying. These numbers are insane and an indefensible waste. That's an insane number and an indefensible waste.

Ali, what do you think?

Ali says

Christine, you make excellent points. If I were to offer career advice, I would strongly suggest that you look at accounting. It's a growing field with opportunities at many different levels. It offers an upward career trajectory. And it's going to become more important as business becomes more global.

Accounting schools place every last person they graduate. Their career counseling isn't about trying to find a job; it's about how to choose among the many firms that are trying to recruit you.

The main growth in accounting is in auditing, born of mergers and acquisitions and international work. At its base, any business that wants to conduct a transaction that involves valuation of that business requires reliable auditing of its books. So there's a massive growth in auditing just by virtue of the fact that the world is shrinking. As trade barriers have fallen by the wayside, there are more international mergers—and that means we need more translation among currencies and countries. Any business that wants to sell itself has to provide audited books; and any acquirer has to believe those books are accurate.

The regulatory environment, too, has spurred a greater need for auditing. Since the financial scandals of the early 2000s and the subsequent passage of the Fair Disclosure law, there's been a greater call for regulation worldwide. And those regulations are changing. We're probably in the middle of a 25-year period of constantly shifting financial regulations, and those changes drive a need for more, and more sophisticated, accounting.

We're also in a world of tax code changes. That puts pressure on businesses and individuals to know how to minimize their taxes, how best to employ their money, or how to get a tax credit on a personal and a commercial basis.

So those are three absolute reasons why accounting as a profession is growing; and it's growing all the way from auditors at the Big Four firms to H&R Block–type companies to off-the-books bookkeepers. So if you're contemplating a midcareer switch, and you have these skills, bookkeeping is actually a pretty good field to go into. And if you're at the high end, go into auditing.

Now, while auditing at a big firm may be a young person's game—get in early and your career track is pretty much set—bookkeeping has a much broader age range. There are small firms in need of those skills; there are the seasonal employers such as H&R Block; and there are even entrepreneurial opportunities, such as part-time bookkeeping for your local deli or helping people with their individual tax returns.

Senator Lamar Alexander (R-Tennessee), a former U.S. Secretary of Education, also supports the three-year degree. He believes it's an especially valid approach for liberal arts majors going into a graduate program, such as medicine, because those young people are going to have a very long course of expensive education.

Senator Alexander's point is that if you know what you want to do, you need to focus at the outset and keep moving. We're in complete agreement. It's a shame that kids often spend a couple of years in college finding themselves before figuring out what they want to do. If high schools did a better job of helping kids identify their strengths, those kids wouldn't spend so much time and money messing around in college.

As we all know, the cost of a college degree keeps rising. And while it's extremely difficult to get a good job without one, a degree is not a promise of employment. Not anymore. Students have to be focused and they can't switch majors too many times. There's no money to go to school for five years at 25 grand a pop. There just isn't.

But there is some good news on the funding front. President Obama, in signing health care reform in 2010, included reform of the student loan system as well. Now, for example, if you want to be a lawyer, you can borrow for your education and your loan will be forgiven if you work 10 years as a public defender. The system is called income-based repayment.

These income-based repayment schedules provide incentives to fill the jobs we really need, such as nurses, rural doctors, and public defenders. We often use the tax code as an instrument of social policy; now we're using the student loan system to try to reward what we require in society.

The recent changes to the student loan system are the most sweeping in history. They take effect in 2014. So if you're a parent with kids in grade school or junior high, you can start to think about focusing them on some expensive degrees that, in the past, you might not have considered. You no longer have to worry that your kids will never pay off their student loans.

These new realities provide an excellent starting point for a parent-child conversation. It should probably take place several times while the kids are in high school, and focus on getting them to assess, realistically, where their skills and interests intersect.

Parents should explain that money isn't infinite and that time is incredibly important. You, Mr. or Ms. Kid, are going to have four years filling your head and your résumé with what you need to get a job, and then you're going to spend the rest of your life at one or more jobs. Start now to find out what you're good at, what someone will pay you for, and what you can reasonably do to live a comfortable life and build wealth.

Thinking of Changing Fields?

So far in this chapter, we've spoken primarily to potential college students and their parents. But education is a much broader topic and addresses a much wider audience. The fact is that none of us should ever stop learning. There are always opportunities for education that will make us more attractive to our current—and potentially future—employers.

Many of us are stuck in jobs we may not like, or in industries that are in decline. If you're among those people, this may be the time to consider your options and to take the steps necessary to transition yourself into a new career.

One area poised for enormous growth is information technology, known by the shorthand IT. IT covers everything from fixing computers to troubleshooting corporate intranets to designing company-specific local area networks. Even more, IT specialists keep corporate America moving. They're responsible for the systems that run the proprietary and third-party programs businesses rely on to function. Clearly, it's a field on the rise and companies will be seeking trained, competent personnel for the foreseeable future.

Another expanding industry is health care. That includes nurses, home health aides, physical therapists, lab technicians, and an extensive list of other occupations having to do with the administration and application of medical services. America is aging. According to the Pew Research Center, an estimated 10,000 baby boomers will turn 65 every day for the next 19 years. Whether they like it or not, they'll be a little less fit and healthy each year. They'll need many different kinds of physical and medical assistance, and the need will only grow.

The good part for you is that you can get into either industry with as little as six months of training. Once in the midst of it, you can see which areas play to your strengths and determine how best to advance. These fields each have established training courses, so you can see how long it takes to be certified in their various specialties. In many cases, you can even take courses online.

Other fields are growing as well. The energy industry will need more workers as we seek to exploit our natural resources more fully. An oil patch roustabout can easily make six figures. Transportation workers, such as truck drivers, also earn high wages.

How to Speak Money—*Talking Points*

Christine says

I'm often asked, "How should I decide what to study? How can I point myself in the direction of a satisfying future?"

Those are good, smart questions. I believe you should study something that you like, something that you're good at, and something that someone will pay you to do. The intersection of those three things is different for every person.

High school career counselors are supposed help you figure this out, but ultimately only the student really knows the right path to take. Ideally, you want to set your course early: College is a really expensive forum for self-discovery.

Training is not difficult and not expensive, and the skill is highly mobile, allowing you to work anywhere there are roads.

Christine remembers her father doing the math when she went to college and showing her how much each class cost every day. With those numbers in mind, she thought twice about skipping class. That kind of discipline is even more important today, because college has become significantly more expensive. Today's graduates have more debt than any other graduating class of college seniors.

Now, don't get us wrong—we both believe that college debt is good debt. On average, a college degree is worth an extra one million dollars over the course of a working life. The only way to turn a student loan into bad debt is by dropping out, taking a low-paying job outside your career field, or by partying your student loan money away.

Mark Kantrowitz, the education guru at FinWeb, says, "If you are taking student loans, you must live like a monk in college." He's right. A generation ago, kids went on spring break with their loan money. Those days are gone. That's just the way it is.

If your child majored in fine arts or philosophy, the only place he or she is really qualified to get a job is ancient Greece.

—*Conan O'Brien, comedian, at an Ivy League commencement*

Surprisingly, some recent studies have indicated that the more an individual worked at a job in high school, the less likely he was to graduate from college. We expected the opposite result. When we were in high school, the people who had jobs—including us—were junior capitalists. But it may be that kids today are working because their families need the money, and they may be dropping out of college for economic reasons.

But we believe that there is a work ethic in high school that needs to be encouraged. We wish that high schools taught more test-taking skills and better study habits and other things that could help kids do a better job in college. Today's kids are entering a much tougher job market and a much tougher *life* market than their parents did. It's even more difficult now than it was for their older brothers and sisters. They're going to need all the help they can get.

In the book *Academically Adrift*, the authors cite a frightening statistic: "Forty-five percent of students did not demonstrate any significant improvement in learning during the first two years of college."

How to Speak Money—*Talking Points*

Ali says

I recently gave a commencement speech to a group of liberal arts graduates from a liberal arts college. My challenge was to make them feel excited about the big wide world waiting for them. The problem is that it's a limited world for liberal arts majors. Competition is keen and jobs are very hard to come by. But I know if there's one place in the world where a kid with a general college education can have any opportunity, it's in the United States.

There's still something that you can't put your finger on about the United States that allows people like Christine and me, who were both liberal arts majors, to succeed. And I think engineers need a liberal arts education, too. It's very important. It's not one or the other; it's both.

A liberal arts education familiarizes an individual with the broader currents around him. In a global marketplace, it's ever more important that we understand history, language, culture, and the commonalities and differences among religions. We have to know about the world, and a liberal arts education teaches us about the world. That's what's so beautiful about it.

In other words, after two years at a four-year college, almost half the students didn't know any more than they did on the day they enrolled. And 35 percent of students did not demonstrate any significant improvement in learning over *four* years of college.

Clearly, too many American kids aren't getting enough out of their college experience. Those years are being wasted, and both the students and the colleges are at fault. College used to be the golden ticket. Once you had the college diploma, you were almost guaranteed a job with growth potential.

College was the magic word on the résumé. The economy was growing, and as long as you could prove that you'd shown up and gotten through a four-year program, companies were happy to place you on the first rung of the corporate ladder. But that was in the days when we were creating 20 million jobs; we're not creating jobs like that anymore.

You might think, therefore, that a liberal arts education is a luxury few can afford. But you'd be wrong. It's true that a liberal arts education, by itself, doesn't qualify an individual for a whole lot of anything. But it turns out that a liberal arts education does provide an appropriate foundation for just about everything.

Again, from *Academically Adrift*, "Students majoring in liberal arts fields see significantly higher gains in critical thinking, complex reasoning, and writing skills over time than students of other fields of study. Students majoring in business, education, social work, and communications showed the smallest gains."

Critical thinking, ability to reason: These are the skills that American corporations need to help them synthesize and analyze vast amounts of information about a global marketplace in which they're trying to sell their products. So we'd say that when choosing between liberal arts and the sciences, choose both. It shouldn't be a question of one or the other; the twenty-first century person needs both.

Your choice of study will have a significant impact on your earnings. As we discussed in Chapter 5, analysis from Georgetown University shows that petroleum engineering majors make a median salary of $120,000, while counseling psychology majors make $29,000.

How to Speak Money's Words to the Wise

1. College (*kol'•ej*): There's no better investment. The earnings differential is staggering. Today, a college degree is a necessary credential. No matter how smart you are, you'll need one to be considered for any kind of corporate position.

2. STEM (*just like it sounds*): The acronym for Science, Technology, Engineering and Math—the disciplines that will lead to high paying, in-demand jobs.

3. Accelerate (*ack•sell'•'r•ait*): Completing a college degree in three years, rather than four, is a good way to save on the cost of education. A growing number of universities are offering accelerated programs to address this need, and many of today's students are taking advantage of them.

7

Speaking Money in the Market

To really build a better future, you can't squirrel your money away under the mattress. That's true even if you sleep in a king-size bed, with plenty of room atop the box springs. Unless you were to sleep upon mountains and mountains of cash, hoarding your savings isn't going to get it done.

If you want to reach financial security, you're going to have to invest. Investing, even if you've never done it before, isn't a difficult concept to grasp. It simply means putting your money to work.

All standard investing falls into one of two categories: *lending* money or *buying* something.

We "lend" through savings accounts, Treasury Bills, and bonds. We "buy" when we acquire stocks. There are many kinds of bonds and many kinds of stocks. There are also many different ways to invest in them safely and sensibly, like mutual funds and exchange traded funds (ETFs). And, for those of us with neither the time nor the knowledge to actively manage our investments, an entire industry of financial advisors has evolved to help us.

Within these broad classes of assets—stocks, bonds, and cash equivalents—there are a host of subcategories. There are government bonds and corporate bonds, and they come with various lengths of time to maturity and rates. In the same way, there are growth stocks and value stocks, and several other ways to choose between companies in which to invest.

You buy some stocks simply for their potential to appreciate in value; you buy others for their steady stream of income through dividends. The simplest explanation is to think of the difference between beef cattle and dairy cows: One gets fattened up and sold when it's grown to the appropriate size. The other is kept around so the owner can enjoy a steady stream of milk for many years.

The financial marketplace has products for every taste and budget. For those seeking safety and security, there are highly-rated bonds. There are blue chip stocks for the sedate Tiffany crowd and stocks of rapidly growing companies for those seeking big payoffs on a small investment.

A blue chip stock is like a high-end retail brand. If you buy one of those stocks, the odds are good that, like a Rolex watch or a vintage Fender guitar, it will increase in value over time. Medium-term government bonds, by comparison, are closer to a department store that offers practical, safe goods—not the most exciting things in the world, perhaps, but they're undoubtedly necessary. The market also offers stocks of small companies and debt instruments from less-developed but fast-growing countries. They bear some similarities to the things you find at those little booths in the middle of the mall, the ones with attractive-looking products of unknown quality. You wouldn't make them the centerpiece of your shopping mission, but you might try one or two since they're priced so well. You could find a real bargain.

Let's focus on the major categories, moving from the most conservative to the most aggressive investments:

- Cash equivalents.
- Bonds.
- Stocks.
- Other.

All publicly traded investment classes in the United States—stocks, bonds, currencies, commodities—are liquid and transparent. That means they are easy to trade and that relevant information about particular holdings is a matter of public record. By law, public companies must file quarterly financial statements with government agencies, must open their books to auditors and must comply with federal regulations designed to protect the investing public.

By understanding each of the asset classes—what they are and how they behave—you'll be better able to determine how they might fit in your own investment portfolio.

Cash Equivalents

Cash money—it sounds solid, tangible, concrete. That's what cash equivalents are. They're highly liquid, very safe investments such as Treasury bills and money market funds that can be easily converted into cash. Because they're so safe, these instruments tend to pay a low rate of interest—risky investments earn the highest returns, and there isn't much risk involved here.

The most common examples of cash equivalents are:

- Savings deposits.
- Certificates of deposit (CDs).
- Money market deposit accounts.
- Money market mutual funds.

When you deposit your money in a bank, as we've noted, you're actually lending it to that bank. The bank, in turn, lends your money to other people, to businesses and to government agencies. They earn interest on those loans and they pay some of that interest to you. Generally, savings vehicles are very safe. With the exception of CDs, which have predetermined time parameters, when you want your money back, you can withdraw it quickly and without penalty.

Even though cash equivalents don't earn a great deal of interest, they are still a safe place to put funds that you may need to access quickly. When you've got more lying around than you can

 How to Speak Money—*Talking Points*

Ali says
During the recession, when everyone was in a complete panic, I stuck to my plan. I continued doing what I'd been doing: staying diversified, rebalancing, and feeling confident that the market would churn ahead as it always has. So far, I've been right.

keep in your top dresser drawer, cash equivalents let you earn something on that money while you're waiting to use it. Investors buy cash equivalents as a temporary parking place while they decide what new investments to make. The key, though, is that they have to be temporary.

Cash equivalents tend to have considerably less capital risk than stocks or bonds. The Federal Deposit Insurance Corporation (FDIC), a federal government agency, insures savings deposits, CDs, and money market deposit accounts for up to $250,000 per account per institution. Although money market mutual funds are not FDIC insured, most are covered by the Securities Investor Protection Corporation (SIPC), a private insurance program.

The most significant risk to cash equivalents is inflation. If it outstrips the interest you're earning from your cash equivalents, your money loses its purchasing power. If, for example, you earn 1 percent from a savings account while inflation is at 3 percent, your money isn't keeping up with the rising cost of goods and services. One hundred dollars in your savings account will grow to $101 by the end of the year, but a basket of goods that costs $100 today will increase in price to $103 over that same period. If that happens, you're $2 away from your financial goals.

Argue Box

Ali says

The worst thing you can do is not take advantage of the opportunities that are right in front of you. Sure, the stock market has its ups and downs, but it remains the single best place for most people to build wealth. The thing is, you have to be willing to pay attention to stay on top of your investments and stay disciplined.

Christine says

Everything in your life has to do with money. People say to me, "Oh, it's Greek to me, I don't understand money. . . ." You're wrong! You do. You have to. It's not about being greedy, it's about making the decisions that will build wealth down the road and make your family more secure. Everybody wants that.

Let's Speak Bonds

A bond is a loan. Whether you buy a municipal bond, a savings bond, or a corporate bond, the underlying premise is the same: You are lending money to an entity (corporate or government) for a defined period of time at a fixed rate of return.

Companies, municipalities, states, and the federal government use bonds to finance many different kinds of projects and activities. In return for your money, the issuer promises to pay you a fixed amount every year for the life of the bond, and to return the entire amount of your loan at the end of the time period.

It's straightforward: The bond itself will state the interest rate (coupon) that will be paid, and state when the loaned funds (bond principal) are to be returned (maturity date). Interest on bonds is usually paid every six months. The main categories of bonds are corporate bonds, municipal bonds, and U.S. Treasury bonds.

The keys to a bond's interest rate are the credit quality of the issuer—whether it can be trusted to pay you back—and the length of time to maturity. Bond maturities range from a 90-day Treasury bill to a 30-year government bond. Corporate and municipal bonds typically have maturities in the 3- to 10-year range.

Bonds are called *fixed income* investments because you know in advance what your return will be. The income is *fixed*. In that sense, a bond is a very safe investment. You know what you will get. That's why bonds are often good for people on fixed budgets who can't afford not to receive a known quantity of money every year.

You don't have to hold on to bonds; you can also sell them before they mature. Perhaps you decide that the return you are earning, while decent, is less than you believe you could get elsewhere, like in the stock market. The bond market is highly liquid, and you can sell your bond easily.

By the same token, you don't have to buy bonds from the issuer alone. Let's say that five years ago, the government issued a 10-year bond paying 7 percent interest. When the stock market is down and inflation is low (for example, when this chapter was written), a 7 percent coupon can look pretty good. You can purchase a pre-owned bond from someone who, for whatever reason, is willing to sell it.

But if that bond is more attractive now than it was when it was issued, you will have to pay more than its face value to obtain that guaranteed 7 percent coupon per year. If it was a $100 bond at issuance, for example, you might have to pay $110 for it. Conversely, if the market for bonds has weakened, you might be able to pick it up for $90.

Price versus Yield

If overall interest rates decline—from 6 percent to 4 percent, for example—your 7 percent coupon is more valuable, because it represents a guaranteed, virtually risk-free rate of return that is significantly higher than an investor could get from a savings account, money market fund, or CD.

If, on the other hand, interest rates rise to 8 or 9 percent, then the bond will be worth less, and its market price will reflect this fact.

If you buy a 10-year $100 bond at par—the price at which it was issued—and it pays an annual return of 7 percent, then you have an actual return—a *current yield,* it's called—of 7 percent. But if prevailing interest rates rise, the price of the bond will decline. Again, this doesn't matter if you do nothing but hold the bond.

But what if you bought the bond "second hand" as it were, for just $90? The 7 percent coupon the bond is based on pays $100 face value and remains fixed. But the current yield—the actual percentage return on *your* investment—is higher than 7 percent. That's because the $7 interest you earn each year (7 percent of $100) is 8 percent of the $90 you paid for the bond.

It's a seesaw: When the price rises, yield declines. When interest rates fall, the bond itself is worth more but its coupon is worth less as a percentage. When interest rates rise, the bond is worth less but the fixed percentage coupon is worth more relative to the bond's cost.

Bonds have at least two kinds of risk. The first is that the bond's coupon rate will slip lower than the current prevailing interest rate or, worse yet, below the rate of inflation. Should that happen—and historically it has—your bonds will be worth less, because the money you'll receive is worth less. (Why is the money worth less? Because it won't buy as much as it once did.) You still earn the promised rate of interest for as long as you own the bond, though, and you're still paid 100 percent of the principal upon maturity, put another way, you're getting less value than you originally expected to get.

Argue Box

Ali says

You have to grow your wealth. The only way to grow it faster than inflation and faster than your wages grow is to be invested in the market in a way that exposes you to upside but limits your downside.

That's a little sophisticated, I know, but you don't really have a choice. You're either going to have to marry rich or win the lottery, or you're going to have to take some degree of calculated risk in the market.

Christine says

You have to have a plan, know your plan, and work your plan. You can't deviate from it when times are tough. The craziness in Washington or in the markets or in the global economy is not something you personally can control. What you can control is where your assets are allocated.

Make sure you're appropriately allocated in both your taxable and tax-deferred portfolios. You need to be in the asset classes that you know and are comfortable with. That requires a little bit of homework, but you can have a professional help you.

Another, and recently more serious, kind of risk is that the corporation, municipality, or other entity issuing the bond will go out of business, lose all its money, be struck by an asteroid, or in some other way default on its obligation to you. This is truly the worst-case scenario.

To protect you, there are rating agencies whose entire mission is to assess the strength of bond issuers. These organizations, such as Moody's, Standard and Poor's, and Fitch Ratings, examine the financial health of the issuers and give them a letter grade: AAA is the highest, next comes AA+, AA, AA–, A+, and so on, down to the letter B. In the cloudy waters below B are high-yield bonds, also called junk bonds.

Junk bonds pay the highest rate of interest, because if they didn't, no one would invest in them. But at a high enough rate of return, someone will be willing to take the risk. Conversely, the more highly rated the institution, the more certain the repayment and the lower the interest rate the bonds will offer.

As we've noted, bond maturities range from 90 days to 30 years. The longer the time frame, the greater is the risk of inflation eating away at the value of returns. To compensate, long-term bonds generally pay higher rates of interest than shorter-term instruments.

Certain kinds of bonds also allow you to collect your interest free of taxes. Municipal bonds, issued by states, counties, and cities to fund public works projects, are typical examples. They're good vehicles for individuals in high tax brackets, where a tax-free 5.5 percent return is better than an 8 percent taxable one, because the government could take up to 40 percent of the return in taxes.

The World of Stocks

Over the long term, stocks have provided investors with the highest average rates of return. They have historically been the engines of the greatest portfolio growth.

Unlike bonds, a stock is not a loan. When you purchase a stock, you are buying part of a company. You become one of many, many owners. You agree to accept the ups and downs inherent in the performance of any business in exchange for a portion of the profits. A great many factors affect a company's profitability—the state of the overall economy; the company's position versus that of its competitors; its labor situation; its cost of supplies, distribution, and advertising; its management team; its financial controls; the legal and regulatory environment—the list goes on and on.

Money is for making things happen.
—*Sir Richard Branson, chairman, Virgin Group Ltd.*

Some people buy stocks for appreciation: That is, they buy because they expect the shares of the company to increase in value. Some people are more interested in income: the dividends that are paid to investors each quarter on every share they own. These dividends represent the profits that the company pays to investors. Like a bond yield, a company's dividend is stated as an actual amount of money per share (for example, on April 21, 2011, General Electric announced a quarterly dividend of $0.33 per share), not a percentage of the stock price.

When the company does well, it increases its dividend payments and shareholders benefit. When selecting stocks, some people actively seek companies known for paying dividends that are higher than other companies in the same category. They decide that the higher dividends are more important to them than a quick appreciation in the price of the stock. After all, generous and predictable dividend payments are a very attractive purchase incentive. The dividends can be useful income. Or, if not spent, they can be reinvested in shares of the company.

Of course, if a company has a bad year, it may cut its dividend or skip paying it altogether. Even in tough times, though, companies are very reluctant to cut or suspend their dividends, because many investors interpret such a move as a sign of deep trouble. They then sell their shares, driving down the value of the company overall.

One disadvantage of owning shares in a company is that you, as an investor, are not well protected against troubles in the company. If the firm ultimately goes bankrupt, you could lose the entire value of your investment.

But let's look at the bright side. It's not just dividends that allow you to benefit from stocks; you also profit when the value of the shares themselves rises. There can be many reasons for a stock price increase: The overall economy is growing and bringing the company along with it; the company's sector—energy, pharmaceuticals, retail, transportation, and so forth—is doing well; the company has a competitive advantage in the marketplace; the company is well positioned to take advantage of seasonal, demographic, or climate-related conditions, and so on.

The constant in all of these examples is the expectation of higher corporate profits. The stock price reflects the public's confidence—or lack of it—in greater earnings going forward.

In fact, the key driver of a stock price is the market's view of a company's near-term earnings. If the market expects good things, the stock rises. If the market expects the company to encounter trouble—for reasons that can range from a declining national economy to problems within the company itself—then the stock price falls.

International Investing

Today, no one market, region, or country consistently outperforms all the others. While the United States is still the world's largest economy, China is gaining rapidly. In fact, many experts believe China will overtake us as an economic power in the next 10 years. Other markets—Europe, India, even Africa—offer opportunities as well.

When you include international stocks and bonds in your portfolio, you increase your ability to take advantage of profitable opportunities wherever they occur. Many of today's fastest-growing companies are located outside the United States.

By broadening your base of countries, you also help protect your portfolio from the effects of a downturn in any one market or region. Savvy investors know that diversification today means more than selecting stocks across different industries; it means investing across different countries as well.

Free trade has made the world a smaller place. Newly opened markets and a growing global middle class have increased the

Argue Box

Ali says

We have to be willing to go outside our comfort zones. We travel because we want exposure to new things; we have to think about that in our investments. We're not little kids, and the world in which we play is substantially bigger than it used to be.

It's very much like language: If you don't understand it, you'll stick to the thing on the menu that you most clearly understand. When it comes to money, you're going to have to learn how to pronounce the things that you don't know how to pronounce; otherwise, you just won't get ahead.

Christine says

Sometimes it's not where you look, it's how you see. A few years ago, I began to notice there would always be four or five Apple product boxes on my street on recycling day.

So I started to follow Apple's stock chart. It was at 30; then it hit 40. Then I noticed a new Apple store—there had been only one, and I noticed they'd opened another. Then they started talking about some new products.

The stock went to 60. I continued to see those Apple boxes on recycling day. As I write this, Apple hit another all-time high, even as we're talking about a slowing economy.

That's a long way of saying that you don't always have to go very far to find opportunity. You just have to be alert for it. There's a lot still to be mined in your comfort zone.

demand for smart phones, computers, automobiles, appliances, and many other goods and services. Banks, retailers, cement companies, and even life insurance companies have sprung up all around the planet, and their hungry consumers allow them to grow much faster than their U.S. counterparts.

Today, 11 of the world's 20 largest companies are headquartered outside the United States. They may do a significant portion of their business here, but home is on another shore. According to *Forbes* magazine, the largest construction, auto, business equipment, and food companies are all non-U.S. firms.

Before the Internet and globalization, it was difficult to obtain accurate financial information on non-U.S. companies. But today, world markets can be accessed by almost anyone, and you can now obtain precise information from Hong Kong, Japan, Russia, Brazil, or any other of the world's exchanges with just a few mouse clicks. Reliable data means that you can buy and sell international investments with a much higher degree of confidence than you could previously.

Investors today also have access to international bonds. Kazakhstan may issue a 20-year bond to pay for the development of a huge gas field so far from any settled territory that it will require the construction of a new city just to house the workers who will ultimately drill there. The Chinese Development Corporation might issue a bond to pay for the construction of a hydroelectric project. The Federal Republic of Germany might float a 15-year bond to cover the cost of safety upgrades to the country's power-generating plants. You get the idea—bonds with varied risk-and-return characteristics are issued to finance many different kinds of projects.

While the specific percentage of assets you should allocate to non-U.S. investments is a very legitimate issue, the question of international investing *per se* has already been answered. That answer is yes. It makes sense for you to follow opportunities wherever they are.

Stepping into the Market

Now that we've discussed the different asset classes, let's talk about the best way to invest in them. Today, there's really no need for an average investor to buy individual stocks, bonds, and bank CDs for one's portfolio.

You can still do so, of course, but it takes a great deal of time, skill, and research to determine which ones are going to perform better than others. And you'd have to pick several securities in each category to avoid the risk of being overly concentrated in any particular investment.

So the financial services industry has developed investment vehicles that make it easy for you to own multiple stocks, bonds, and cash equivalents with a single dollar. These vehicles are mutual funds, index funds, and exchange traded funds—better known as ETFs.

Funds, whether actively or passively managed, are the right investment choice for most individual investors. Mutual funds, index funds, and ETFs can provide diversification within asset classes, bring you access to opportunities around the globe and offer expertise in unfamiliar markets.

Mutual Funds

You probably already know something about mutual funds. They're the most common investment vehicles on the planet. But just to clear up any misconceptions and to make sure we're all starting on the same page, let's quickly go over a few of the basics.

A mutual fund pools money from hundreds and thousands of investors to construct a portfolio of stocks, bonds, real estate, or other securities, according to its charter. Each investor in the fund gets a slice of the total pie. One unit of the mutual fund provides a piece of every holding within the fund. Whereas $100 might get you 10 shares of a particular stock, $100 invested in a stock mutual fund will give you a smaller share in the 20 or more stocks that the fund invests in.

In this way, a mutual fund provides ready-made diversification for each dollar invested. Most funds require only moderate minimum investments, from a few hundred to a few thousand dollars, so you can construct a diversified portfolio much more cheaply than you could on your own.

Before you invest in a mutual fund, check its expense ratio. You need every possible bit of your return—you don't want to give too much of it to the mutual fund company. The expenses may not seem like much—no more than a few percentage points a year—but they create a serious drag on performance over time.

Taxes, too, can negatively affect your return. If your fund owns dividend-paying stocks, or if the fund manager sells some big winners, you'll owe your share of Uncle Sam's bill.

Look for Consistency in Style and Performance; Don't Chase Returns

Remember, it's important to find the funds that match your goals. It's silly to chase today's leading performers, because funds that rank highly over one period may not finish on top in later ones.

Look for consistent, long-term results and a stable investment style. If you've selected a small-cap stock fund, be sure the manager isn't dabbling in large-cap stocks just to boost the fund's return. It may seem good for the mutual fund, but so-called "style drift" can distort your overall asset allocation and risk profile.

Index Funds

Here's an expression we bet you've heard: "If you can't beat 'em, join 'em." That's the idea behind index funds. Index funds don't try to outperform their various market benchmarks—the S&P 500, the Dow, the Nasdaq, and so forth. Rather, they seek to replicate them.

Unlike actively managed funds, these funds are "passive"—there's no manager deciding what to buy. Because of that, index funds tend to charge lower expenses and be more tax efficient (they don't incur the tax liabilities caused by constantly selling stocks within the fund), and there's no risk the fund manager will make sudden changes that throw off your portfolio's allocation.

How to Speak Money—*Talking Points*

Christine says

I have six months of my living expenses in savings. That's just liquid cash. Then I have an E-trade account invested in plain vanilla ETFs that's managed based on a pie chart for my age. Like my savings, it's also available if I need it quickly.

And then my real investments—where I am the most diligent about investing—are in my husband's and my 401(k)s. And those are never going to be touched until I'm all gray, I hope.

John C. Bogle, the founder of the Vanguard Group, is the individual most responsible for the creation of index funds. He realized that investors were being hurt three ways by traditional actively managed mutual funds.

First, investors' desire to always achieve the best returns ultimately wounded them. They'd chase a successful manager and then, when her star had faded, seek another. Buying and selling funds cost money, and very few managers could provide superior returns for extended periods.

Second, the fund's expenses—the costs involved in having these managers actively buy and sell securities—often took 2 percent or more off the top of a fund's return. If a fund returned 10 percent, investors made eight. Third, the churning of the fund—the constant buying and selling of securities as it frantically sought high returns—generated trading costs that were passed along to investors and, in addition, generated capital gains on which taxes had to be paid.

Bogle had an idea: Instead of trying to beat the market, why not match it? If the S&P 500—a market-weighted basket of the stocks of 500 leading U.S. companies—returned an average of 10 percent per year, why not create a fund that mimicked it? All you'd have to do, he reasoned, was purchase the same stocks in the same proportion as the S&P 500. So he did.

The Logic of Index Funds

Almost from Day One, the index fund was a resounding success. There wasn't the constant buying and selling that characterized actively managed funds. Bogle rarely touched his fund, making changes only when the S&P did. The fund wasn't always spinning off tax-generating capital gains, nor was it filled with charges and fees that cut into returns like an axe.

Because it didn't cost a lot of money to manage the fund—just assemble the basket and leave it alone—the ratio of expenses to assets was only 0.18 percent: just 18 one-hundredths of a single percentage point. Investors kept much more of their return than they did with actively managed funds, and over time, thanks to the power of compounding, that money added up.

Soon other index funds were created. Some tracked the Dow. Some replicated the Russell 2000, which tracks small-cap

Argue Box

Ali says

I'm frustrated with people who say they don't understand money and don't understand investing, but who have never made any effort to learn. I would suggest to you that investment risk—people's biggest fear—goes down exponentially based on how much you learn about how money works. Once you have a basic understanding it's a lot less scary.

Christine says

We're always speaking money, even when we're not saying a word, by the choices we make. And you may think, "Oh, I don't speak money, I'm not fluent in it," but you are. You're speaking it all the time. Every decision you make has financial implications. So make sure that you're saying what you want to say.

companies. Other funds were created to bring index investing to bond funds. Today, there are hundreds of index funds that track sectors, industries, countries, regions, and entire markets around the world.

There's another reason so-called "index" investing makes sense in so many situations: The majority of the return earned by stock and bond funds does not depend on the skill of the individual manager; it's driven more by the overall direction of a given market, industry or geographic region. Yes, there are disciplines in which manager skill is key to success—hedge fund investments, for example. But in the general stock and bond markets, a rising tide lifts all boats and a hurricane batters both the good and the bad.

There are some caveats. Indexing seems to work best in large transparent markets, like those for U.S. stocks and bonds. Because there is so much information on these big securities, it's tough for a fund manager to gain an edge on the market. But in emerging markets, or in newer industries such as alternative energy or genetically enhanced foods, or in a particular far-off emerging market, the story may be different. In those instances, certain managers may have access to detailed information that others don't, and they can act on this information to produce superior returns.

Exchange Traded Funds (ETFs)

Exchange traded funds are index mutual funds that you buy and sell just like stocks. Want to invest in the market quickly and cheaply? ETFs are the most practical vehicle. All the major stock indexes have ETFs based on them, including the Dow Jones Industrial Average, the Standard & Poor's 500 Index and the Nasdaq Composite.

ETFs have been called the most innovative investment product of the past 20 years. They offer many of the benefits of standard index funds—low costs relative to other investments, tax efficiency, diversification, transparency—but they have other advantages as well.

For starters, ETFs can expose you to opportunities that were formerly too difficult to access. Large-cap stocks in Japan? Sure. Timber and mining companies in Indonesia? No problem. Technology in Scandinavia? You got it. Today, you can get ETFs that track broad-based indexes, international and country-specific indexes, industry- and sector-specific indexes, bond indexes, and commodity indexes. There are ETFs for large U.S. companies, small ones, real estate investment trusts (REITs), international stocks, bonds, and even gold. Pick an asset class that is publicly available, and there is a good bet that it is represented by an ETF or will be soon.

ETFs are economical to buy and especially to maintain over the long run, making them especially attractive for the typical investor. Annual fees are as low as .09 percent of assets, which is breathtakingly low compared to the average mutual fund fees of 1.4 percent. You could build an entire, well-diversified portfolio using nothing but ETFs.

Because ETFs are sold through brokers, you have to pay a transaction fee to purchase them, but they're still not expensive relative to other investments.

Do Your Homework!

It goes without saying (but we'll say it anyway) that you owe it to yourself to do some research before you put your money in any investment. In-depth mutual fund information is widely available, either from the funds themselves, from third-party ratings companies or by using CNNMoney.com's mutual fund screening tool. Just to review, here are some things to look out for:

1. *Invest in funds with low expenses.* Fund expenses directly reduce your returns, so you'll increase your odds of success by avoiding funds with bloated expense ratios.
2. *Look for consistency of style.* For a fund to fit into a diversified portfolio, it's important that the manager stick to a particular investing style. If you bought a fund because you want your portfolio to include, say, small value stocks, then you don't want a fund manager jumping into large stock issues.
3. *Consider risk.* Returns may vary, but funds that are risky tend to stay risky. So be sure to check out the route the fund took to rack up past gains and decide whether you would be comfortable with such a ride.
4. *Check out past performance relative to peers.* If you're investing in an actively managed fund rather than an index fund or ETF, you should look at its long-term record (at least three

How to Speak Money—*Talking Points*

Ali says

When you don't speak somebody's language, in finance or in life, then situations can become so fraught with tension that you're not always able to comprehend your own thoughts, let alone someone else's.

But if you can learn to understand your business partner or your life partner or your spouse, your roommate, your brother, your sister, your parents—if you can just get out of your own way and understand where someone else is coming from, and why, then it's easier to accept their opinions as simply THEIR opinions. You don't have to share theirs, and they don't have to share yours. But they—and you—need to hear one another.

I don't buy this business about money being inaccessible. It's not inaccessible to everybody. And if you can learn to speak it, you'll get a lot more input and you'll make better decisions.

years and preferably five) compared to that of its peers and to category averages. It's hard to be forgiving if a fund does much worse than all its peers, especially if it does so over a sustained period.

5. *Seek low taxes.* You can't forget about taxes just because you don't have any intention of selling your fund shares. As a fund owner, you also own all the stocks in the fund's portfolio. If the fund manager sells a stock for a huge capital gain, you'll have to report that gain on your tax return. This doesn't apply to gains in a tax-sheltered retirement account, like an IRA or 401(k).

6. *When investing in stock funds, steer clear of asset bloat.* This is more of an issue with small-cap funds. Since they invest in companies with very few shares, an extra two billion from new investors like you can tie the manager's hands. To put the additional money to work, the manager might have to drop his standards or accumulate overly large positions in individual stocks.

7. *When investing in bond funds, stick with short-to-intermediate bond maturities.* Over the past 20 years or so, long-term bond funds have provided the highest returns, but that may not always be the case. What's more, long-term bond funds can be surprisingly volatile. If interest rates rise just 1 percentage point, a long-term bond fund can drop 10 percent or more, wiping out more than a year's interest.

8. *Beware of tempting bond yields.* Fund companies know that investors focus on yields. So some do everything they can to pump up yields. If you can't understand why a fund has MUCH higher-than-expected returns, move on (or accept the fact that you're investing in a riskier-than-average fund). A lot of Madoff investors wished they had followed this simple piece of advice.

How to Speak Money's Words to the Wise

1. Marketplace (*mahr'•kit•plaess*): The markets are where all the world's trends are evaluated, priced, and auctioned. From the value of a corporation to the future value of a bushel of wheat, from the creditworthiness of a mid-sized American city to the currency of a sovereign nation, the world trades every minute of every business day.

2. Instruments (*In'•struh•mintz*): There are more financial products available today than ever before. We have access to large-, mid- and small-cap stocks; short-, intermediate-, and long-term bonds; mutual funds; and ETFs, as well as to more esoteric vehicles for more sophisticated investors. Whether through a bank or brokerage, or on your own on the Web, you can find investments that will fit your objectives, your time frame, and your tolerance for risk.

3. Advisor (*ad•vye'•z'r*): Very few people have the time or the expertise to track the universe of investment opportunities. A professional investment advisor can help you construct a portfolio designed to address your specific return, risk, and time objectives. There are many kinds of advisors, who perform different functions and have different ways of pricing their services. It may be worth considering an advisor to assist you in reaching your goals.

Speaking Money to Investment Principles

Markets move in cycles. They go up, they go down, and they go up again to a new high. Picture a mountain peak, a valley, and then another, higher mountain peak—that's a market cycle. So even when we're in a deep trough—a recession—we can assume that the market will ultimately recover. Because that's what the market has done since commerce began.

But more than that, financial markets behave according to a set of defined principles. The more you understand about money, the better you'll be able to speak it. So let's talk about the principles that govern the markets.

Principle 1: There Is a Direct Relationship between Risk and Return

The most basic rule of investing is this: Risk and reward go together. The asset classes with the best long-term performance also have the greatest year-to-year fluctuation in value.

That fluctuation—called *volatility*—is what makes certain asset classes risky: In the short term, you never know what you're going to get.

Let's look at the three major categories of investments: stocks, bonds, and cash equivalents. Assume you'd placed $100 in each of these three categories 40 years ago. How much would your investment be worth today?

It's not even close! You can see in Figure 8.1 that the performance of large and small stocks leaves bonds and cash in the dust.

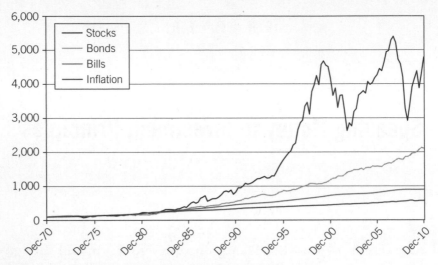

Figure 8.1   Stocks, Bonds, Bills, and Inflation, 1970 to 2010
Source: Lipper, 2011. All rights reserved. Used by permission.

Your $100 stock investment has grown to $4,780—almost two-and-a-half-times the value of your bond purchase, which is now worth $2,101. Your cash equivalents have grown to only $898. Inflation, meanwhile, has taken $573 from the value of each of those returns. So over the long term, despite the occasional blips and hiccups, stocks have clearly bested all other asset categories and kept well ahead of inflation.

But looking year to year, it's a different story.

Look at those ups and downs. Figure 8.2 shows that from one year to the next, stocks are very volatile—if you need your money in a hurry, there's no guarantee you'll have as much as you invested. You would lose money if you had to take it out of the market while the market and your stocks are down.

Over time, the market pays you a premium for accepting a higher degree of uncertainty about how your investment will perform in any given year. So the longer your time frame, the riskier you can afford to be.

About now, you're probably wondering, "What's a typical return for a typical year?" You may also be asking yourself, "What about those bad years? How much can I lose?" Both are good, smart questions.

Within the universe of stocks, shares of large companies—large-cap stocks—are the most predictable performers. Over the 82 years

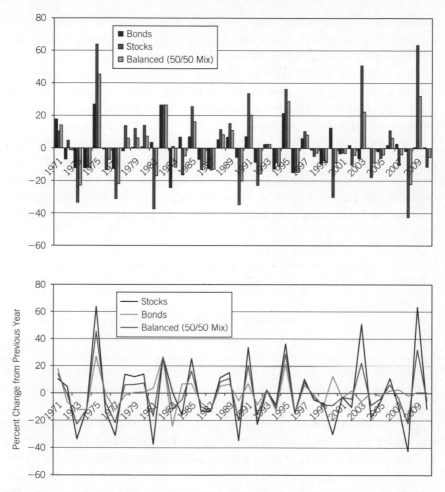

Figure 8.2   Year-Over-Year Fluctuations in Returns among Stocks, Bonds, and a Balanced Portfolio, 1970 to 2010

from 1928 to 2010, they have produced an average total return of 11.3 percent.

Though that sounds pretty good, it doesn't tell the whole story. The ride to that 11.3 percent average can be mighty bumpy. In the best single year for large-cap stocks, they returned 54 percent. But in the worst year ever they *lost* 54 percent. Ouch! That's volatile.

The concept of volatility is an extremely important one. It's what people mean when they talk about market risk. With large-cap stocks, the risk isn't that the company will go out of business; it's that you can't predict from one year to the next what your return will be, so it's risky to plan on anything specific.

To evaluate risk, investment professionals use a measurement called a *standard deviation*. A standard deviation indicates how far your investment's returns are likely to vary from their historical average two-thirds of the time.

So, when statistics show that large-cap stocks have an annual average return of 10 percent with a standard deviation of 20 percent, it means that four years out of six you can expect returns between 30 percent on the high side and –10 percent on the low end of the scale. You'll be plus or minus 20 percentage points from 10 percent.

Investing is laying out money today to receive more money tomorrow.
> —*Warren Buffet, chairman, Berkshire Hathaway Inc.*

In the case of large-cap stocks, then, 20 percent on either side of the average return represents one standard deviation from the average return.

What about those other two years out of six? When considering more extreme futures, you should be prepared for results of 10 percent plus or minus as much as 60 percent, or a range from 70 percent to –50 percent, which includes outcomes for three standard deviations from the average return (this will account for about 99.7 percent of probable returns).

Every asset class—from large-cap stocks to government bonds to international stocks—has its own average risk-and-return coordinates. We can plot them on a graph, making *return* the *y* axis (the vertical line) and *risk* the *x* axis (the horizontal line).

Let's take a look.

There, that's clearer. In Figure 8.3 you can see the 30-year risk-and-return characteristics for four major asset classes, represented here by mutual funds: U.S. Large-Cap Core Funds, U.S. Small-Cap Core Funds, General U.S. Government Funds (long-term), and Short-Term Government Bonds (maturities of three years or less). We've also shown inflation.

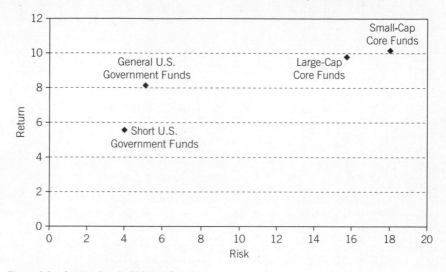

Figure 8.3   Scatter Graph: Risk and Return

One glance shows you how it works. The higher the return, the greater the risk. The less certain the earnings in any given year, the greater your earnings over the long term.

And if you're thinking that the lower return doesn't look so bad, given the safety of the investment, it can be a different story once you consider the effects of inflation.

Over the past 30 years, inflation has averaged 4.5 percent per year. That means if you have a paper return of 8 percent, your purchasing power increased by only 3.5 percent. If you earn 5 percent, you really get 0.5 percent. If your statement says you've made less than 4.5 percent, you've lost purchasing power. So if you were counting on bonds or Treasuries to protect your future, you could find yourself underwater just when you were counting on a safe, dry retirement.

Here's a critical question: When will you need to take your money from the market and start using it? If it's next year, you'll have to think twice about stocks, because who knows what they'll be worth in such a short time frame. You'd have a better chance of earning a positive return in bonds, and you'd have the best chance in cash, although at current interest rates, you won't get much of a return.

1Y Returns

	Large-Cap Stocks	Small-Cap Stocks	Bonds	Bills
Max	37.6	51.8	32.6	15.0
Min	−37.0	−35.3	−10.8	0.1
Range	74.6	87.1	43.4	14.8

	Large-Cap Stocks	Small-Cap Stocks	Bonds	Bills
12/31/1970	3.9	−21.45	2.5	6.58
12/31/1971	14.3	16.57	20.2	4.41
12/31/1972	18.99	9.83	13.4	4.15
12/31/1973	−14.69	−26.38	1.3	7.26
12/31/1974	−26.47	−24.15	−10.8	8.11
12/31/1975	37.23	51.8	16.1	5.94
12/31/1976	23.93	36.23	15.6	5.1
12/31/1977	−7.16	17.34	3.04	5.39
12/31/1978	6.57	19.28	1.39	7.42
12/31/1979	18.61	39.4	1.93	10.53
12/31/1980	32.5	31.88	2.71	12.02
12/31/1981	−4.92	−0.29	6.25	14.97
12/31/1982	21.55	24.71	32.62	11.12
12/31/1983	22.56	28.36	8.36	8.94
12/31/1984	6.27	−6.19	15.15	9.94
12/31/1985	31.73	30.23	22.1	7.73
12/31/1986	18.66	6.92	15.26	6.15
12/31/1987	5.25	−4.01	2.76	5.93

5Y Returns

	Large-Cap Stocks	Small-Cap Stocks	Bonds	Bills
Max	28.6	32.2	18.4	11.5
Min	−2.4	−10.9	3.1	2.1
Range	30.9	43.1	15.4	9.4

	Large-Cap Stocks	Small-Cap Stocks	Bonds	Bills
12/31/1974	−2.38	−10.90	4.77	6.09
12/31/1975	3.20	1.65	7.41	5.96
12/31/1976	4.89	4.87	6.58	6.10
12/31/1977	−0.19	6.26	4.56	6.35
12/31/1978	4.35	17.03	4.58	6.39
12/31/1979	14.82	32.18	7.40	6.86
12/31/1980	14.02	28.51	4.80	8.06
12/31/1981	8.13	20.74	3.05	10.01
12/31/1982	14.12	22.22	8.39	11.19
12/31/1983	17.36	24.02	9.84	11.50
12/31/1984	14.81	14.58	12.55	11.38
12/31/1985	14.67	14.29	16.51	10.51
12/31/1986	19.87	15.90	18.42	8.76
12/31/1987	16.46	9.99	12.53	7.73
12/31/1988	15.31	8.64	12.43	7.31
12/31/1989	20.36	13.36	12.31	7.02
12/31/1990	13.20	3.99	9.78	7.04
12/31/1991	15.36	9.95	9.92	6.91

20Y Returns

	Large-Cap Stocks	Small-Cap Stocks	Bonds	Bills
Max	17.9	17.2	10.6	7.9
Min	8.2	9.3	6.9	3.4
Range	9.7	8.0	3.7	4.5

	Large-Cap Stocks	Small-Cap Stocks	Bonds	Bills
12/31/1989	11.56	11.21	9.21	7.82
12/31/1990	11.17	11.62	9.54	7.88
12/31/1991	11.91	12.70	9.35	7.94
12/31/1992	11.35	13.03	9.05	7.90
12/31/1993	12.78	15.70	9.49	7.69
12/31/1994	14.60	17.25	9.95	7.50
12/31/1995	14.61	16.22	10.06	7.48
12/31/1996	14.57	15.57	9.46	7.48
12/31/1997	16.66	16.03	9.81	7.47
12/31/1998	17.76	14.77	10.19	7.34
12/31/1999	17.88	13.87	10.04	7.06
12/31/2000	15.68	12.94	10.50	6.76
12/31/2001	15.24	13.40	10.61	6.20
12/31/2002	12.71	11.23	9.59	5.72
12/31/2003	12.98	11.79	9.37	5.32
12/31/2004	13.22	13.13	8.83	4.90
12/31/2005	11.94	12.05	7.88	4.67
12/31/2006	11.80	12.48	7.35	4.59

Date				
12/31/1988	16.61	20.72	7.89	6.87
12/31/1989	31.69	16.01	14.53	8.43
12/31/1990	-3.1	-15.41	8.96	7.83
12/31/1991	30.47	41.28	16	5.53
12/31/1992	7.62	16.33	7.4	3.51
12/31/1993	10.08	17.52	9.75	3.05
12/31/1994	1.32	-1.04	-2.92	4.32
12/31/1995	37.58	27.2	18.47	5.64
12/31/1996	22.96	21.82	3.63	5.18
12/31/1997	33.36	26.99	9.65	5.17
12/31/1998	28.58	-4.15	8.69	4.87
12/31/1999	21.04	19.14	-0.82	4.72
12/31/2000	-9.1	12.02	11.63	5.94
12/31/2001	-11.89	8.19	8.44	3.48
12/31/2002	-22.1	-15.37	10.25	1.61
12/31/2003	28.68	42.06	4.1	1.03
12/31/2004	10.88	19	4.34	1.38
12/31/2005	4.91	7.53	2.43	3.07
12/31/2006	15.79	15.3	4.33	4.67
12/31/2007	5.49	0.34	6.97	4.4
12/31/2008	-37	-35.27	5.24	1.4
12/31/2009	26.46	32.18	5.93	0.15
12/31/2010	15.06	25.5	6.54	0.14

Date				
12/31/1992	15.88	14.25	10.90	6.42
12/31/1993	14.55	13.64	11.28	5.65
12/31/1994	8.70	10.09	7.66	4.83
12/31/1995	16.59	19.44	9.48	4.40
12/31/1996	15.22	15.96	7.04	4.34
12/31/1997	20.27	18.01	7.48	4.67
12/31/1998	24.06	13.29	7.27	5.04
12/31/1999	28.56	17.58	7.73	5.12
12/31/2000	18.33	14.63	6.46	5.18
12/31/2001	10.70	11.94	7.43	4.83
12/31/2002	-0.59	3.21	7.55	4.11
12/31/2003	-0.57	11.66	6.62	3.34
12/31/2004	-2.30	11.64	7.71	2.67
12/31/2005	0.54	10.73	5.87	2.11
12/31/2006	6.19	12.15	5.06	2.34
12/31/2007	12.83	16.03	4.42	2.90
12/31/2008	-2.19	-0.85	4.65	2.97
12/31/2009	0.41	1.26	4.97	2.72
12/31/2010	2.29	4.43	5.80	2.13

Date				
12/31/2007	11.82	12.73	7.56	4.52
12/31/2008	8.43	9.27	7.43	4.24
12/31/2009	8.21	9.98	7.01	3.83
12/31/2010	9.14	12.17	6.89	3.45

Figure 8.4 Reduction of Risk over Time (Range of Returns in 1-Year, 5-Year, and 20-Year Periods)

Source: Lipper, 2011. All rights reserved. Used by permission.

But if you have 5 or 7 or 10 years, or even longer to wait, then it's a different story.

Let's look at our next principle of investing.

Principle 2: Time Is Your Friend

Historically, time smoothes out volatility. So the longer you stay in the market, the more likely you are to see your investment perform according to expectations.

Let's take a look at how the range of returns narrows when we hold our investments for a longer period of time.

When you look at Figure 8.4, you can see that even the most volatile asset class, small company stocks, becomes relatively stable when you take the long view. So, if you have a reasonable time horizon, you have an excellent chance of high average returns over many years. And that translates into a comfortable retirement with plenty of cushioning along the way.

But let's say you don't have such a long time horizon. Let's assume you're approaching retirement. Perhaps you're already in retirement. How can you get the returns you want while minimizing the volatility you don't want? The answer can be found in one word: *diversification*.

Principle 3: Diversification Lowers Your Risk and Improves Your Return

In simplest terms, diversification is the investment version of the saying, "Don't put all your eggs in one basket." A diversified portfolio spreads your investment among multiple asset classes to help protect you from downturns in any one area.

While markets move in cycles, individual asset classes generally don't move in the same direction at the same time. So by blending different classes in your portfolio, you can earn steadier returns.

To get the benefits of diversification, you want assets that aren't closely *correlated* to one another. *Correlation* is a measure of how similarly two asset classes perform. If they're too similar—if they go up and down more or less in tandem—you're not getting much diversification out of owning both of them. On the other hand, if every time one goes up the other goes down, then you've got great diversification.

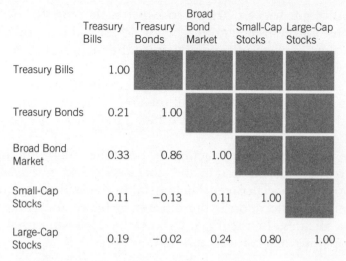

	Treasury Bills	Treasury Bonds	Broad Bond Market	Small-Cap Stocks	Large-Cap Stocks
Treasury Bills	1.00				
Treasury Bonds	0.21	1.00			
Broad Bond Market	0.33	0.86	1.00		
Small-Cap Stocks	0.11	−0.13	0.11	1.00	
Large-Cap Stocks	0.19	−0.02	0.24	0.80	1.00

Figure 8.5   Correlation Can Help Evaluate Potential Diversification

In Figure 8.5, you can see how different asset classes correlate to one another. All correlations are set between 1.00 and −1.00. A correlation of 1.00 means an asset class moves the same amount in the *same* direction at the same time as another. A correlation of −1.00 means an asset class moves the same amount in the *opposite* direction at the same time as another. In real life, asset classes achieve a perfect 1.00 correlation only to themselves; and there are no asset classes that exhibit perfect negative correlation.

Diversification doesn't just lower volatility; it can actually improve your earnings. The different asset classes enhance one another, balancing each other while they smooth your progress toward your goals.

Think of a great band—maybe Brad Paisley's, if you're so inclined, or Led Zeppelin if you're of a certain age, or even Lady Gaga's back-up group (not that they get much notice). Each musician brings different skills to the total enterprise. You've got a drummer who's as solid and dependable as a rock. Your bass player gives you the bottom that allows the guitar and the horns to soar above. The guitarist not only provides the cross-rhythms that keep things interesting, he plays the leads that bring the crowd to its feet. You've got back-up singers to sweeten the sound. And you've got horns, synthesizers, and maybe an occasional harp or fiddle to squeal, blurt, wail, and fly so high above the melody that the laws of gravity seem to disappear.

It's a wonderful mix, because each group member brings his individual strengths to the overall mission. They complement each other; they don't replicate each other. That's what noncorrelated diversification is about.

The science of constructing a portfolio—determining how much to put into cash, bonds, and stocks—is called *asset allocation.*

The difference between kitchen table diversification and professional asset allocation is the difference between a garage band and the Beatles. In theory, it's the same idea—music—but one group operates at a considerably higher level.

Asset Allocation: The Key to Results

According to something called modern portfolio theory, the way you combine your assets is the key to how much you earn. It's much more important than what you buy or when you buy and sell it. So it's not necessary to chase the hot stock tip or the brilliant money manager. You don't have to spend energy trying to figure out the best time to buy or sell. It's more productive to construct a portfolio with the blend of assets that's right for your individual situation.

Those who ignore asset allocation do so at their peril. Some experts believe that it accounts for more than 90 percent of the difference in performance between one portfolio and another.

 Your Three Key Steps

1. Diversify.
2. Allocate.
3. Optimize.

The beauty of the theory is that it makes investing easier. The most important thing isn't whether you choose between Home Depot and Lowe's; it's that you have a portfolio that contains stocks, bonds, and other investments: It's the blend of asset classes that counts.

Adding stocks to a bond portfolio increases return and lowers risk. In fact, a portfolio divided equally between stocks and bonds has approximately the same risk as an all-bond portfolio and provides substantially more return.

It's mathematically possible for you to combine different asset classes so that your portfolio gets the highest potential return for each unit of risk you choose to accept. The portfolio is then said to be on the efficient frontier—it has the best possible ratio of return to risk. Take a look at Figure 8.6. It shows something called the "Efficient Frontier" that explains how diversification can help lower your risk and increase your return:

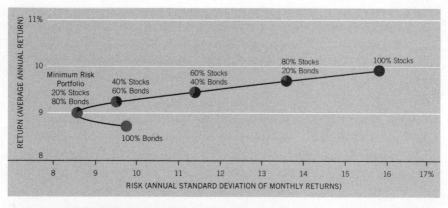

Figure 8.6   Efficient Frontier: Diversification Can Help Lower Risk

Sources: BlackRock®; Informa Investment Solutions. Past performance is no guarantee of future results. It is not possible to invest directly in an index. Investing involves risk. **Stocks** are represented by the S&P 500 Index, an unmanaged index that consists of the common stock of 500 large-capitalization companies, within various industrial sectors, most of which are listed on the New York Stock Exchange. Stock prices fluctuate with market conditions and may result in loss of principal. **Bonds** are represented by the Merrill Lynch U.S. Treasuries 10+ Year Bond Index, an unmanaged index that includes U.S. Treasury securities with maturities of greater than 10 years. Bonds held to maturity offer a fixed rate of return.

The information shown is for illustrative purposes only and is not meant to represent the performance of any particular investment. Diversification does not guarantee a profit or protect against loss.

At that point, to continue our music analogy, your portfolio is now the New York Philharmonic under the direction of James Levine. Every string, woodwind, and brass instrument; every tympani, triangle, and bell is playing in such beautiful harmony that the audience, rapt, finds itself transported to an emotional plane it never even knew existed.

Unless your portfolio is already optimal, it can be made more efficient through careful and disciplined asset allocation. This is an area in which a good professional advisor can add real value.

How to Speak Money's Words to the Wise

1. Principles (*prin'•sa•pulls*): Investing is not magic. There are solid principles that underpin investment success. By putting these principles—the relationship between risk and reward, for example, or the relationship between time and volatility—into action, you can increase the likelihood of meeting your wealth-building objectives.

2. Characteristics (*kair•ik•tur•iss'•tiks*): Different asset classes perform differently at different points in a market cycle. Economic and fiscal conditions that favor bonds, for example, may hurt the performance of stocks. To build a portfolio that will perform consistently through a wide range of conditions, experts recommend a mix of stocks and bonds, and different categories of each.

3. Time (*thai'm*): Time is your friend. It smoothes the effects of volatility—the year-to-year fluctuations in performance of a given asset. The longer you hold an investment, the more likely it is that the investment will perform to its historical average.

CHAPTER

9

Speaking Money in Your Own Portfolio

We've seen that there are smart ways to invest in any asset class. And we know that combining asset classes is the best way to ensure a steady return on your investments. Furthermore, we've learned that even volatile assets do well over time (in fact, they produce the best long-term performance).

So the strategy you follow should be a function of your investment time horizon—how many years you'll be contributing to your portfolio before you start taking money out of it—and your ability to tolerate volatility, or risk. After all, you've got to be comfortable with the decisions you make.

To help you decide what's best for your situation, we've asked Doug Flynn, certified financial planner, and Richard Zito, certified financial planner, to create five model portfolios for us. (Mssrs. Flynn and Zito are the co-founders of Flynn Zito Capital Management LLC, a registered investment advisor.) Each portfolio corresponds to a certain set of life criteria, but the two key determinants of the appropriate portfolio for you are your age and your personal level of tolerance for risk.

We'll define the five investor segments by risk tolerance and portfolio objectives, like this:

Very High Risk Tolerance (Aggressive Growth)
Most suitable for those with the longest time horizon (under age 34) who focus on the highest long-term growth without regard for investment income and who can tolerate

potential loss of principal in exchange for the potentially highest returns.

High Risk Tolerance (Growth)

Most suitable for those with a long time horizon (ages 35 to 44) who focus on strong growth without regard for investment income and who can accept some declines in value in exchange for potentially higher returns.

Moderate Risk Tolerance (Growth with Income)

Most suitable for those with a medium-term time horizon (ages 45 to 54) who seek moderate growth and stable income, and who can tolerate small drops in value during difficult market conditions.

Low Risk Tolerance (Income with Moderate Growth)

Most suitable for those with a shorter time until retirement (ages 55 to 64) who seek cautious growth and steady income and who find it difficult to tolerate portfolio declines.

Very Low Risk Tolerance (Income)

Most suitable for investors near or in retirement (ages 65-plus) who are focused on stability, small profits, and the protection of principal.

Let's start with a simple self-test to assess which portfolio will be most appropriate for your situation. This test comes to us courtesy of LPL Financial, a Registered Investment Advisor, but we'll call it the Christine-Ali Test (because Christine won the coin toss), and it will—we hope—help you make decisions from a more informed perspective.

Your Investment Questionnaire

The test has 15 questions, divided into three sections: your time horizon, your investment goals, and your tolerance for risk.

Each answer is awarded one to four points. The one point answer is always at the top of each question; the highest point answer at the bottom. At the end of the test, you'll multiply your answers in the first section by one, in the second section by two and in the third section by three. You'll add the totals for each section to determine your overall number, and that number will help you decide which of our model portfolios will be most suitable for your situation.

I. Time Horizon

What is your age?
56 and over	1
46 to 55	2
36 to 45	3
20 to 35	4

What is your primary financial goal?
Wealth preservation	1
Retirement planning	2
Wealth accumulation	3

What is the time frame for you to achieve your financial goals?
0 to 5 years	1
5 to 10 years	2
10 years or longer	3

Time Horizon Total _____

II. Financial Goals

Which of the following best describes your financial goals?
Preserving principal and earning a moderate amount of current income	1
Generating a high amount of current income	2
Generating some current income and growing assets over an extended time frame	3
Growing assets substantially over an extended time frame	4

How do you expect your standard of living five years from now to compare to your standard of living today?
Lower than it is today	1
The same as it is today	2
Somewhat higher than it is today	3
Substantially higher than it is today	4

Five years from today, you expect your portfolio value to be:
Portfolio value is not my primary concern; I am more concerned with current income	1
The same as or slightly greater than it is today	2
Greater than it is today	3
Substantially greater than it is today	4

Generating current income from your portfolio is:
A primary concern (only if you are about to retire)   1
Not important   2

With the income generated from your portfolio, you plan to:
Use it for living expenses   1
Use some and reinvest some   2
Reinvest it all   3

Financial Goals Total _____

III. Risk Tolerance

You have just received a windfall of $50,000. How would you invest it?
In something that offered moderate current
    income and was very conservative   1
In something that offered high current
    income with a moderate amount of risk   2
In something that offered high total
    return (current income plus capital appreciation)
    with a moderately high amount of risk   3
In something that offered substantial
    capital appreciation even though it has
    a high amount of risk   4

Which of the following statements would best describe your reaction if the value of your portfolio were to suddenly decline by 15 percent?
I would be very concerned because I cannot
    accept fluctuations in the value of my portfolio   1
If the amount of income I receive was
    unaffected, it would not bother me   2
Although I invest for long-term growth, I would
    be concerned about even a temporary decline   3
Because I invest for long-term growth,
    I would accept temporary fluctuations
    due to market influences   4

Which of the following investments would you feel most comfortable owning?
Certificates of deposit   1
U.S. government bonds   2

Blue chip stocks   3
Stocks of new or high growth companies   4

Which of the following investments would you least like to own?
Stocks of new or high growth companies   1
Blue chip stocks   2
U.S. government bonds   3
Certificates of deposit   4

Which of the following investments do you feel are the most ideal for your portfolio?
Certificates of deposit   1
U.S. government securities   2
Blue chip stocks   3
Stocks of new growth companies   4

How optimistic are you about the long-term prospects for the economy?
Very pessimistic   1
Unsure   2
Somewhat optimistic   3
Very optimistic   4

Which of the following best describes your attitude about investments outside the United States?
Unsure   1
I believe the U.S. economy and foreign
   markets are interdependent   2
I believe overseas markets provide
   attractive investment opportunities   3

Risk Tolerance Total _____

INVESTOR SCORECARD

Time Horizon Total ___ × 1 = _____
Financial Goals Total ___ × −2 = _____
Risk Tolerance Total ___ × 3 = _____
TOTAL SCORE _____

(Note: The total for each section is multiplied by a number that represents the overall importance of that section when determining your investment objectives.)

Match your total score with one of the investment objectives listed below. If your score is near the top or bottom of an adjusted total range, you may want to examine the next or previous objective to determine which represents your needs more accurately.

Adjusted Total Range	Investment Objective
34–57	Income with Capital Preservation
58–83	Income with Moderate Growth
84–99	Growth with Income
100–114	Growth
115 –125	Aggressive Growth

The investment objectives shown are for illustrative purposes only. Your investment objective is based on many factors, including your financial situation, tolerance for risk, time horizon, and other financial needs. Consult your financial advisor if you have any questions.

Income with Capital Preservation

- Need for capital preservation and current income
- No focus on growth
- Lowest tolerance for risk
- Shortest investment horizon

Income with Moderate Growth

- Need for current income
- Moderate focus on growth
- Low tolerance for risk
- Short or intermediate investment horizon

Growth with Income

- Equal focus on growth and current income
- Moderate tolerance for risk
- Intermediate investment horizon

Growth

- Little need for current income
- Focus on growth
- High tolerance for risk
- Intermediate or long investment horizon

Aggressive Growth

- No need for current income
- Focus on aggressive growth
- Highest tolerance for risk
- Long investment horizon

Remember, there are no right or wrong answers to any of these questions. Except for your age, the questions are completely subjective—they're about your attitudes and expectations. A further caveat is that each of us uses words differently. One person's interpretation of moderate growth or small losses may be unlike another's. So this test is only a guide to get you thinking about the implications of the decisions you will make. No matter how you answered, you did great.

Your Model Portfolios

Now let's take a look at some investment portfolios tailored to the investment objectives we've just identified (shown in Figures 9.1 to 9.5). We asked two professional money managers, Doug Flynn, certified financial planner, and Rich Zito, certified financial planner, to develop model portfolios appropriate for each of the five profiles, from the most conservative to the most aggressive. Mr. Flynn and Mr. Zito, who co-founded Flynn Zito Capital Management LLC, a registered investment advisor, prepared the following allocations:

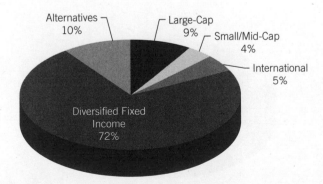

Figure 9.1   Income with Capital Preservation (Lowest Risk)
Source: Flynn Zito Capital Management LLC.

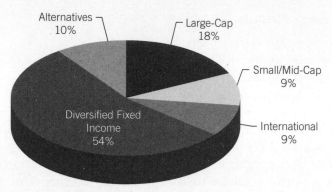

Figure 9.2   Income with Moderate Growth (Low Risk)
Source: Flynn Zito Capital Management LLC.

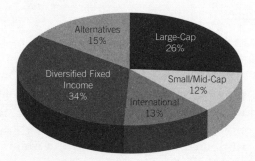

Figure 9.3   Growth with Income (Moderate Risk)
Source: Flynn Zito Capital Management LLC.

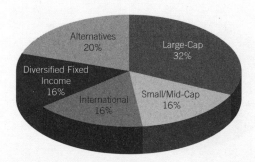

Figure 9.4   Moderately Aggressive Growth (High Risk)
Source: Flynn Zito Capital Management LLC.

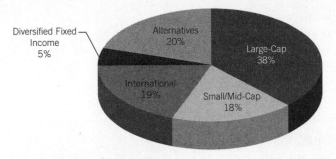

Figure 9.5   Aggressive Growth (Very High Risk)
Source: Flynn Zito Capital Management LLC.

All of our portfolio pie charts have five slices. What makes the portfolios different is the pie-specific weighting assigned to each of the categories. Every slice, though represented as a single entity, encompasses several different subcategories. To give you a fuller sense of the discipline involved in creating the portfolios, we list the kinds of securities contained in each.

Large-, Mid-, and Small-Cap Equity

1. Core/blend
2. Growth
3. Value

International Equity

1. Foreign large/mid/small-cap
2. Core/blend
3. Growth
4. Value
5. Developed emerging markets
6. Developing emerging markets

Diversified Fixed Income

1. Aggregate (core) bonds
2. Government bonds (Treasuries and agencies)
3. Corporate bonds (investment grade and high yield)
4. Municipal bonds (investment grade and high yield)
5. Strategic income (multisector and flexible income)
6. Foreign bonds (hedged, unhedged, and emerging market)
7. Inflation protected securities (taxable and tax-free)

8. Floating rate/bank loans
9. Long/short credit (unconstrained)
10. Master limited partnerships (MLPs)
11. Preferred stock
12. Convertible securities

Alternative Investments

1. Commodities
2. Currencies
3. Real estate/REITS
4. Private equity
5. Absolute return
6. Market neutral

You can see that the portfolios contain all the asset classes we've discussed, except for cash. That's because we've assumed your cash is sitting on the side, in a separate account where you can take what you need when you need it. (For beating inflation, cash doesn't work for you all that well.)

You can use these models as a general guide in creating your own portfolio. Simply fill in the slices of the pie with the investment vehicles you choose and you're on your way. They can be active funds, index funds, or ETFs. You can build a portfolio from your company's 401(k) offerings.

If you're building your portfolio with mutual funds, though, remember that you might not be able to use the fund's name to determine in which slice it belongs. You can check the mutual fund screener at CNNmoney.com to see the fund's actual category.

You can—and sometimes should—have more than one fund in each category, but you should do it to diversify, not duplicate, your other holdings. For example, if you have an S&P 500 index fund, you probably don't also need a large-cap stock fund. But owning both a transportation stock index fund and a retail stock index fund makes more sense, because they'll have different holdings.

The Importance of Rebalancing

We'd suggest you review your portfolio every quarter. Pick a comfortable time and comfortable chair and look over your account. The key is to leave emotion out of it—whether they're up or down, quarterly returns are too short-term to get excited about. But it's important to stay involved with your finances. After all, it's your future we're talking about. Don't make rash decisions, but don't be afraid to change. And please, don't do something just because your brother-in-law did. Your portfolio is for you. Tailor it to your individual situation.

While you should review your portfolio each quarter, you'll probably want to rebalance it once a year. You'll want to make sure your portfolio addresses the person you are, not the person you were.

Remember that both you and your portfolio will change as time goes by. You'll get older and your time until retirement will grow shorter. And not every slice of your portfolio pie will grow at the same rate. So it's a good idea to examine your portfolio each year and rebalance your assets in light of those changes. There are two reasons to do this:

1. Your portfolio assets will grow at different rates.
2. Your risk tolerance will change over time.

If, for example, you allocated 8 percent to small- and mid-cap stocks and they grew so fast that they're now 11 percent, take some of that money and move it so that the actual portfolio composition is in line with your objectives. It's hard to sell winners; your natural instinct is to buy more of them. But to maintain the proper portfolio balance, there will be times when you'll have to sell assets that go up and buy the ones that didn't.

It's not just your age that can change your risk profile. You'll want to adjust your portfolio mix to reflect your evolving goals. Marriage, a child, a home—life isn't static. Investing isn't static, either. So ride herd on those investments—don't let them stray off the trail.

Financial Advisors—Yes or No?

Many people wonder about the use of financial planners or financial advisors. We think these professionals can play an important role in helping us create more orderly plans and make better financial decisions.

The sheer volume of financial products on the market today is staggering. Without the time or the expertise to evaluate the myriad offerings available, it's easy to make choices that, ultimately, turn out to be less than ideal. This is where a trained, experienced financial advisor can be most valuable: She is a resource, an educator, a confidante who can guide you in establishing a plan that fits your objectives, time frame, and investment parameters.

Many of us are quite willing to hire carpenters to modernize our kitchens, trainers to buff us up and, of course, barbers and hairdressers to help us stay well groomed.

But when it comes to the most important decisions about arguably the most important area of our lives—our futures—the attitude is often, "Why should I pay some joker to do something I can do myself?"

The truth is, you probably can't do it yourself. Not well, anyway. If you fix the kitchen sink and it still doesn't drain quite right, it may not be that big a deal. And if you give junior a bad haircut, it will grow out in just a couple of weeks. But if you plow ahead and invest in stocks and bonds with no previous experience and your portfolio underperforms by a significant margin, you're throwing away your best chance for a better life.

How many millionaires do you know who have become
wealthy by investing in savings accounts? I rest my case.
—*Robert G. Allen, Canadian-American financial writer*

That's why we believe that it makes sense to engage a professional who knows the terrain and whose job it is to help you walk a safe and comfortable path to long-term financial security.

Financial planners can help you access opportunities you might not otherwise know about. They can discuss your investments with the insight and nuance gained from working with individuals at all different levels of experience and understanding. They can help you optimize your portfolio, keep you on track, coach you through the tough times, and commend your ultimate success.

Many different kinds of professionals make up the universe of advisors. There are straight commission brokers, who earn a fee on every trade you make. The more you trade, the better they do. There are fee-based professionals who will manage your portfolio for a small percentage of the assets in it. There are those who charge by the hour, like an attorney, and who will listen to your questions, assess your situation, and provide advice. There are discretionary managers to whom you give the power to trade on your behalf, and there are arrangements in which you must give approval to every move up front.

Only you can decide, which, if any, of these avenues might make sense for you. If you're more comfortable doing your own research (and there's plenty of information publicly available) and executing your own trades, by all means do so. If you're the kind of person who would appreciate a professional point of view, well, that's certainly available, too.

Before you commit to any particular advisor, here are some questions you might want to ask him:

1. *What experience do you have?*

    How long has the planner been in practice? How much experience does he have helping individuals with their financial needs?

2. *What are your qualifications?*

    Look for a planner who has proven experience in investments or retirement planning. Ask what licenses and certifications the planner holds, and what steps he takes to stay current with changes in the field.

    The most important thing, though, is that the planner has the training and skill to provide assistance in your individual case, and that planner is someone with whom you feel comfortable.

3. *What services do you offer?*

    The services a financial planner offers depend on credentials, licenses, and areas of expertise. Some planners offer advice on a range of topics but do not sell financial products. Others may provide advice only in specific areas, such as estate planning, tax matters, or insurance.

4. *What is your approach to financial planning?*

    Make sure the planner's viewpoint is neither too cautious nor too aggressive for you. Some planners require you to have a certain net worth before offering services. Find out if the planner will carry out the financial recommendations developed for you or refer you to others who will.

    Most planners will ask many of the questions we've asked here. They'll want to know your goals, your risk tolerance, your personal, family, and business situation. The degree of customization they offer in their planning may vary.

Some planners take a holistic approach, looking at the totality of a client's financial life—insurance, taxes, estate planning, and more. Others focus exclusively on a single area, such as portfolio management. Still others put clients with similar goals, investment time horizons, or wealth levels into the same basket of securities—essentially, model portfolios in which a few sizes fit all (as we showed last chapter). You may have to meet with several planners before you find one with the appropriate fit for you. Take the time to get it right.

5. *Will you be the only person working with me?*

The financial planner may work with you himself or have others assist him. You'll want to meet everyone who will be working with you. If the planner works with professionals outside his own practice (such as attorneys, insurance agents, or tax specialists), get a list of their names to check on their backgrounds.

6. *How do you charge for your services?*

As part of your financial planning agreement, the planner should clearly tell you in writing how she will be compensated for the services to be provided. As we've noted, it can be by salary from the planner's company, fees, hourly rates, commissions, or a combination of any or all of these.

7. *How much do you typically charge?*

While the amount you pay the planner will depend on your particular needs, the financial planner should be able to provide you with a cost estimate based on the work to be performed.

8. *Are there any potential conflicts of interest in our working together?*

Financial planners who sell insurance policies, securities, or mutual funds have a business relationship with the companies that provide these products. The planner may also receive business for referring you to an insurance agent, accountant, or attorney. There's nothing necessarily bad in these arrangements; it's simply that if they exist, the planner should inform you of them.

9. *What professional organizations do you belong to?*

Several government and professional organizations, such as FINRA (formerly NASD), your state insurance and securities departments, and certified financial planner board keep records on financial planners and advisors. Contact these groups to conduct a background check.

There's nothing unusual in performing these checks, so please, make the calls. The planner himself may provide references for you. After all, if he's helped others succeed in the markets, isn't that a good advertisement? Conversely, if you hear damaging stories from past customers or a professional organization, you'll want to proceed with caution, if at all.

10. *Can I have it in writing?*

Ask the planner for a written agreement that details the services to be provided. Keep this document in your files for future reference.

By the way, a good planner will tell you most of these things without your having to ask. And almost all planners and advisors will meet with you for an introductory consultation—usually lasting about an hour—at no charge. All you'll invest, initially, is your time.

How to Speak Money's Words to the Wise

1. Profile (*proh'•fyle*): What are your goals? What is your investment time frame? What's your attitude toward risk? What's your tax situation? Answering these and similar questions will help you develop your investment profile, which defines the investment vehicles and investment strategies that will be most appropriate for your individual circumstances.
2. Criteria (*krye•teer'•ee•uh*): What's important when evaluating an investment? What are the key metrics? There are literally hundreds of benchmarks for comparing funds, managers, and vehicles. To us, the consistency of results is more telling than one year of spectacular returns.
3. Advisor (*ad•vye'•z'r*): Very few people have the time or the expertise to track the universe of investment opportunities. A professional investment advisor can help you construct a portfolio designed to address your specific return, risk, and time objectives. There are many kinds of advisors, who perform different functions and have different ways of pricing their services. It may be worth considering an advisor to assist you in reaching your goals.

Speaking Money on the Home Front

"To buy or not to buy: That is the question."

That's how Shakespeare might have put it if he had considered the housing issue instead of writing *Hamlet*.

You probably know that the housing market is in the worst shape we've seen in decades. Prices have declined from the record highs they reached in late 2006 to levels last seen in 1998. We've lost 10 years of housing gains.

Vacancies are at an all-time high. Foreclosure rates are stubbornly high. How did this happen and what does it mean for you?

How it happened goes like this. In the early 2000s, our country experienced a housing bubble. Government policies encouraged home ownership and banks gladly lent to almost anyone who could sign a mortgage document. Interest rates were low, and "no money down" became a mantra. With more people looking to buy homes, prices rose. Then people borrowed against the rising value of their properties, putting themselves deeper in debt but figuring it was safe to do so, since property values kept going up, up, and still higher. Developers jumped in with both feet, increasing the available housing stock. Then the economy began to slow down.

The first to feel it were the low folks on the totem pole. They'd had no business buying homes in the first place, and banks had been foolish to lend to them. But the banks didn't own the loans anymore. They'd sold those loans to investment firms that bundled thousands of loans together, sliced them into thin *tranches*, and sold those tranches to pension funds, foreign countries, and other institutional investors, including other banks. When the marginal individuals at the bottom of the pile began defaulting on their mortgages, it began a cascade of trouble that roared through the entire global economy. Interest rates rose, putting more stable borrowers at risk of default. They'd been comfortable paying an adjustable rate mortgage of x, but when it suddenly became $1.5x$, or $2x$, the story changed.

And as interest rates climbed and money grew tight, no one wanted those big expensive houses anymore. Home values began to slide. Then they began to plummet. Soon many people found themselves with homes worth less than their mortgages. When this happened, houses were said to be *underwater*; that is, the paper value of the property, as reflected in the mortgage, was more than anyone would pay for the property now. Faced with this reality, many homeowners simply walked away.

So, today, we have a country filled with unoccupied houses that are worth substantially less than they once were. With unemployment high and the job market wheezing, people are reluctant to commit to buying a home. And even if they were willing to take the plunge, banks have become much more stringent in their lending policies.

Let's look at the pros and cons. The most basic fact is this: You have to live somewhere. Unless you're staying with your parents or crashing on a friend's sofa, that means paying money for a place of your own.

Whether renting is better than buying depends on many factors, particularly how fast prices and rents rise and how long you stay in your home. An article in the May 11, 2011, issue of the *New York Times* suggested that buying was a more economical decision assuming you stayed in your residence more than five years.

The allure of home ownership is that, in time, the place will be yours. You pay a monthly mortgage (and, if you're living in a condo or co-op, you also pay a maintenance or management fee), but at the end of some finite period, you own it. You can turn around and sell it if you want to, or, once you've paid off your mortgage, you can simply live there without having to pay anything each month.

Given those benefits, why would anyone ever rent? Because, historically, it's been less expensive. Renting is good for people who can't really afford to buy, who don't have sufficient credit history to get a mortgage, or who don't plan to stay in the house or apartment for very long.

Argue Box

Ali says

This is *the* once-in-a-lifetime opportunity to buy a house. Affordability is incredible. You look across the country and prices are down 30 and 40 percent from their peaks. Interest rates are so low that people are getting mortgages for 4 percent, or 5, or 5 and a quarter for even a big mortgage—that's just unbelievable. Rates won't stay this low. Neither will home prices.

Christine says

You don't buy a house because mortgage rates are low, and you don't buy a house because prices are low; you buy a house because you need the house to live in, you've got money in the bank, and this is a good opportunity for you. What if you're a young worker who wants to be mobile? Are you going to be able to sell that house when you're offered a promotion in another city?

What's a good rule of thumb for a mortgage? What you pay for housing—be it rent, mortgage, or mortgage plus maintenance—should not exceed 30 percent of your take-home pay (or 36 percent of your gross). Anything above that is dangerous.

When thinking about how much you can afford, it's important to keep in mind not only the rent or mortgage payments but also all the other costs of running a household. These expenses include taxes, insurance, utilities, household operations (cleaning supplies, postage stamps, and the like), home furnishings and equipment, household maintenance and repairs, yard and garden supplies, and expenses related to remodeling or home improvements.

A house or apartment isn't really a liquid asset. You can sell it if you own it, but it could take you a while to do so. According to statistics, 40 percent of homes sell within one month, and an additional 34 percent sell within the next three months. So in four months, almost three out of every four homes for sale get sold.

But that's a national average, and real estate is locality-specific. In some areas of the country—parts of Florida, Nevada, and Arizona, for example—many properties have been on the market for more than a year.

Buying a Home

If you do want to buy, though, here are a few pointers to keep in mind.

Start by Sprucing Up Your Credit

Since you most likely will need to get a mortgage to buy a house, make sure your credit history is as clean as possible. A few months before you start house hunting, get copies of your credit report. Certify that the facts are correct, and fix any problems you discover.

Credit reports are kept by the three major credit agencies: Experian, Equifax, and TransUnion. Among other things, they show whether you are habitually late with payments and whether you have run into serious credit problems in the past.

A credit score is a number calculated from a formula created by Fair Isaac based on the information in your credit report. You have three different credit scores, one for each of your credit reports.

A low credit score may hurt your chances for getting the best interest rate, or getting financing at all. So get a copy of your reports and know your credit scores. Try Fair Isaac's MyFICO.com, which charges $15.95 each for reports and scores from Equifax and TransUnion. Experian scores and reports can be accessed from experian.com and cost $15.

Errors are not uncommon. If you find any, you must contact the agencies directly to correct them, which can take two or three months to resolve. If the report is accurate but shows past problems, be prepared to explain them to a loan officer.

Aim for a Home You Can Really Afford

Next, you need to determine how much house you can afford. The rule of thumb is that you can buy housing that runs about two-and-a-half times your annual salary. But you'll do better to use one of many online calculators to get a handle on how your income, debts, and expenses affect what you can afford.

For a more accurate figure, ask to be preapproved by a lender, who will look at your income, debt, and credit to determine the kind of loan that's in your league. If you have significant credit card debt or other financial obligations like alimony or even an expensive hobby, then you may need to set your sights lower.

The size of your down payment will also determine how much you can afford.

If You Can't Put Down the Usual 20 Percent, You May Still Qualify for a Loan

If you haven't already, you'll need to come up with cash for your down payment and closing costs. Lenders like to see 20 percent of the home's price as a down payment. If you can put down more than that, the lender may be willing to approve a larger loan. If you have less, you'll need to find loans that can accommodate you.

Various private and public agencies—including Fannie Mae, Freddie Mac, the Federal Housing Administration, and the Department of Veterans Affairs—provide low down-payment mortgages through banks and mortgage companies. If you qualify, it's possible to pay as little as 3 percent up front. For more, check out www.hud.gov, or www.fha.gov.

A warning: With a down payment under 20 percent, you will probably wind up having to pay for private mortgage insurance (PMI), a safety net protecting the bank in case you fail to make payments. PMI adds about 0.5 percent of the total loan amount to your mortgage payments for the year. So if you finance $200,000, your PMI will cost $1,000 annually.

Once you've considered the down payment, make sure you've got enough to cover fees and closing costs. They can easily add up to more than $10,000—and often run to 5 percent of the mortgage amount.

If your available cash doesn't cover your needs, first-time homebuyers can withdraw up to $10,000 without penalty from an individual retirement account. You can also receive a cash gift of up to $13,000 a year (the limit for 2011) from each of your parents (a total of $26,000) without triggering a gift tax.

Check on whether your employer can help. Some big companies will chip in on the down payment or help you get a low-interest loan from selected lenders. You can also tap a 401(k) or similar retirement plan for a loan from yourself, but do this with extreme caution!

Don't Buy a Home without Professional Help

Despite all the tools available today, from books and magazines to online advice, we believe it would be foolish to go it alone. Housing markets are local, and each state, city, and even neighborhood has

Argue Box

Christine says

How good is the school district? What's the commuting distance? What is the viability of the economy in that neighborhood? What are the taxes? I think you always want to look for a property that has room for improvement because that helps you in both your tax base in terms of not buying at the top. I don't think you want to be the biggest or most expensive house on the block.

Ali says

Generally, I encourage people to use a professional agent, but do it with the understanding that you have different interests, and that yours are longer term and involve a lot more dollars. Real estate agents are in the business of moving inventory, and you're not. So while you're on the same side as your agent, you don't necessarily have the exact same interests.

a thicket of local laws or customs that you need to understand. For that, it helps to have a team of professionals to guide you.

You might want to start by finding an agent who can represent your interests in the search. This is not as simple as it sounds. Sure, 85 percent of sellers list their homes through an agent—but those agents are working for the seller, not you. They're paid based on a percentage, usually 5 to 7 percent of the purchase price, so their interest will be in getting you to pay more.

What you need is what's known as an exclusive buyer agent. Sometimes buyer agents are paid directly by you, on an hourly or contracted fee. Other times they split the commission that the seller's agent gets upon sale. In most markets, a buyer's representative has the same access to homes for sale that a seller's agent does, but her allegiance is supposed to be only to you.

A house is a machine for living in.
—*Le Corbusier, architect, designer, and urbanist*

There are now about a dozen websites that help connect buyers with buyers' agents, among them HomeGain.com, House.com, RealEstate.com, and Reply.com.

Next, start looking for a mortgage lender. Take your time, since you could be paying this loan for 30, or even 40 years. Start on the Internet at places like LendingTree.com and E-loan.com. You may also want to check out the rates at CNNMoney.com, Bankrate.com, or HSH Associates. These sites carry nationwide listings of mortgage interest rates and other related information.

Don't limit your search to the Web, though. Once you have an idea of the best rates from national lenders, get on the phone to your community banks and any other institutions with which you may have a relationship. The local lender can often offer a better deal simply because he or she knows the local market.

You might also consider using a mortgage broker, who keeps tabs on rates from a multitude of lenders. Though the mortgage broker is paid by the bank, the fee—usually 1.5 to 3 percent of the loan amount—may get transferred to you in the closing costs. Most search engines have extensive listings of mortgage brokers, but check with other borrowers you know for a recommendation.

Start the Hunt

Your first step here is to figure out what city or neighborhood you want to live in. (Remember the old saw about "location, location, location.")

For overall demographics and data on metropolitan areas, you can visit a city site like Money Magazine and CNNMoney .com's annual Best Places to Live list. For more detailed neighborhood information, check out sites like Trulia.com, Zillow.com, or NeighborhoodScout.com for comprehensive school and demographic information on a number of communities. Look for signs of economic vitality: a mixture of young families and older couples, low unemployment, and good incomes.

Pay special attention to districts with good schools (high teacher-student ratios and graduation rates are among the hallmarks), even if you don't have school-age children. When it comes time to sell, you'll find that a strong school system is a major advantage in helping your home retain or gain value.

Try also to get an idea about the real estate market in the area. For example, if homes are selling close to or even above the asking price, that shows the area is desirable. Try Homegain.com, which is free, or Dataquick.com, which is available only to paid subscribers, to check out recent home sales.

Incidentally, if you have the flexibility, consider doing your house hunt in the off-season—generally, the colder months of the year. You'll have less competition and sellers may be more willing to negotiate.

If you're a first-time buyer, pay special attention to condominiums and cooperatives, or co-ops. Condos generally sell for 15 percent to 20 percent less than the cost of comparable detached homes in the same neighborhood, so you get much more space for your money. Co-ops are usually priced even lower.

What's the difference between the two? In a condo, each owner has absolute ownership of his own unit, which may be an apartment or townhouse. Owners pay a monthly fee to maintain shared areas like the lobby, the pool, or the laundry room. The chief financial risk to a condo owner is that the common charges can rise, or, in the event of a major problem such as a roof repair or boiler replacement, the condo board can assess fees to cover expensive repairs.

How to Speak Money—*Talking Points*

Ali says

We have got to understand that everybody except Americans are urbanizing. It's a more efficient way to live. People consume less energy per capita. They transport things more cheaply. They use public transportation, drive small cars, and live in a reasonably small amount of space.

As energy, transportation, and gas prices continue to skyrocket, it will become crippling to heat a 6,000-square-foot house and drive 35 miles to work. Everybody will try to sell their suburban, 6,000-square-foot house, and they won't be able to get their value for it. Meanwhile, one-bedroom apartments in Manhattan never go down in price, because there's always somebody who's coming in to buy it. People are going to live where the work is.

When considering a condo, find out how much the common charge has changed over the past five years, and whether there have been major assessments during that time. Also ask what percentage of the residents actually owns their units as opposed to just renting them (many condos include both). A complex with lots of renters has fewer owners who care about the upkeep, and it may be harder to get a loan on such a property.

A co-op is a rarer animal limited to major metropolitan areas, especially New York City. Essentially, the complex is a corporation in which each owner is a shareholder. In other words, a co-op owner is a partner in a building, rather than an outright owner of a specific unit within that building.

As with a condo, check on the group's financial health, whether shareholders have been hit with special assessments recently, and whether the unit includes many renters.

When you actually start touring homes, bring a notebook and a digital camera to help you remember details. Your real estate agent should supply you with a description of each house and the lot it sits on, the property tax assessment, the asking price, and sometimes a diagram of the rooms. Your camera and notebook are there to record other details, ranging from the cost of heating to the view out the rear window.

One note: Don't automatically reject a house just because it doesn't measure up to your desires, either in features or price. You can always add a deck, for example, or update a kitchen (even though, as Christine points out, adding a kitchen may add more value to your life than it will to your home). Since the asking price is just a starting point for negotiation, you will be making offers and counteroffers as both parties seek an acceptable price.

Close the Deal

There's no foolproof system for negotiating a fair price. It's occasionally best to deal directly with the seller yourself. More often it's better to work exclusively through intermediaries. In general, don't let the other side begin to believe you are negotiating in bad faith or being deceptive—any deal you eventually reach has to involve trust on both sides.

Be creative about finding ways to satisfy the seller's needs. For example, ask if the seller would throw in kitchen and laundry appliances if you meet his price—or take them away in exchange for a lower price. Remember, too, that your leverage depends on the pace of the market. In a slow market, you've got the advantage; in a hot market, you may have none at all.

Once you reach a mutually acceptable price, the seller's agent will draw up an offer to purchase that includes an estimated closing date (usually 45 to 60 days from acceptance of the offer).

Have your lawyer or agent review this document to make sure the deal is contingent upon:

1. Obtaining a mortgage.
2. A home inspection that shows no significant defects (make sure you're clear on the definition of *significant*).
3. A guarantee that you may conduct a walk-through inspection 24 hours before closing. This last clause allows you to check the home after the sellers have moved out so that you have time to negotiate payment for repairs, just in case the movers cause any damage, or that big living room sofa was hiding a hole in the floor.

You also need to make a good-faith deposit—usually 1 percent to 10 percent of the purchase price—into an escrow account. The seller will receive this money after the deal has closed. If the deal falls through, you will get the money back only if you or the home failed any of the contingency clauses.

Now call your mortgage broker or lender and agree on terms, if you have not already done so. Decide whether to go with the fixed-rate or adjustable-rate mortgage and whether to pay points. For most people, a fixed-rate mortgage, especially at today's rates, is the much smarter option.

If you don't already have one, look into a homeowner's insurance policy, too. Ask for recommendations from friends, your lawyer, or your real estate agent. Most lenders will require you to have homeowner's insurance in place before they'll approve your loan.

In addition to the mortgage lender's appraisal of the house you plan to buy, you should hire your own home inspector. Again, ask for referrals, or check with the American Society of Home Inspectors, a trade group.

Try to be present during the inspection, because you will learn a lot about the house: its overall condition, construction materials, wiring, and heating.

If the inspector turns up major problems, like a roof that needs to be replaced, then ask your lawyer or agent to discuss it with the seller. You will want the seller to fix the problem before you move in, or deduct the cost of the repair from the final price. If the seller won't agree, you may decide to walk away from the deal. You can do it without penalty if you have that contingency written into the contract.

About two days before the actual closing, you will receive a final HUD Settlement Statement from your lender that lists all the charges you can expect to pay at closing.

Review it carefully. It will include things like the cost of title insurance that protects you and the lender from any claims someone may make regarding ownership of your property. The cost of title insurance varies greatly from state to state but usually comes in at less than 1 percent (in Iowa, as little as 0.1 percent plus a fixed fee) of the home's price.

The lender might also require you to establish an escrow account, which it can tap if you fall behind on your mortgage or property tax payments. Lenders can require deposits of up to two months' worth of payments.

After all this rigmarole, the actual closing is often somewhat anticlimactic, though perhaps still nerve-wracking. It's a ritual affair, with customs that differ by region. Your lawyer or real estate agent can brief you on the particulars.

Rent versus Buy: One Man's Story

Not everyone wants to buy. Take a look at 23-year-old Xander Clark. He's got a good job, savings in the bank, and he's got good credit. Still, he decided to rent when he moved to Baltimore.

He said, "I thought about purchasing a home. But I knew that in my line of work, I have to be able to relocate. So this gives me flexibility and mobility." It also gives him a luxurious apartment in a building with a full-service concierge and an outdoor pool. And he doesn't have to mow his lawn.

"I have friends now that are trying to sell their homes," he said. "It's been on the market for a year, and they're not getting the price they're asking. It's scary to think you have to keep lowering the price. Why would I buy something?"

Doug Bibbie, the president of the National Multi-Housing Council, said, "We're seeing a lot of people opting out. They don't want to buy now. They can afford it, but they're betting that housing prices will move lower, or they're betting that they'll be able to change their job."

Xander Clark works in the human resources of a large, name-brand department store. He said, "I could get a promotion and have to move to another city, and they would give me six weeks. I can't afford to be stuck with a house I can't sell."

Renting is also a reasonable option for people who want a community with good schools, but who can't afford to buy there. We see that happening in Chicago, in New York, and on the West Coast.

According to numerous surveys—and this is no surprise—most of us would like to own our homes and live in them with our immediate families. But for millions of people, it makes sense to rent while they repair their financial situations. These people may also decide to live with their parents or children while they work to get themselves on a more solid financial footing. With everyone sharing rent, the task becomes easier.

But demographic trends suggest that not everyone sees the nuclear family—mom, dad, 2.1 kids, three cars, and a dog—as the American dream anymore. The recent census shows that in many parts of the country, multiple generations live together because they want to, not because financial circumstances dictate it. It's an interesting trend—we're moving from *Leave It to Beaver* to *The Waltons*.

What If You're Selling?

We've been talking about buying a home, but sellers have issues and questions as well. When you decide to sell, the first thing to do is investigate the local housing market.

Consult the large real estate sites, like Realtor.com, Zillow.com, and HomeGain.com to see how similar homes are priced in your neighborhood. Many newspapers also list the selling and asking prices of recent sales, plus how long the houses were on the market. Note the prices for your neighborhood during the last several months.

Check how sales were running, say, a year ago, so you get an idea of whether the market is heating up, cooling down, or staying put. This exercise should give you a sense of what your home is worth.

Selecting an Agent

Get an agent. You may decide that you can sell your home without one, since you'd save the 6 percent commission that a broker typically collects. But balance that against the work involved in advertising a house and being available at all hours to show it. We know people who've done well selling their own home, but it takes research and dedication.

Ask for referrals from friends or check the Web and local newspapers for advertisements. Make an appointment with an agent and interview her for the job.

Evaluate the person as though you were a buyer: Is she professional and personable? Does she say the right things to make you want to see the home? Also, since the agent will likely be able to advise you on a selling price, how well does her price jibe with the homework you did on your own? Don't be fooled by an agent who is merely flattering you with an inflated price. Go by what you already know about your house and the current housing market.

Ask whether she will be the agent actually showing the house. Some brokers have specialists whose main duty is to win the listing. Then another of the broker's agents takes over.

The Lowdown on Commissions

Once you find an agent you like, you'll sign a listing agreement, a contract laying out the specifics of your arrangement, such as how long the agent will represent your home and what the compensation will be.

When you discuss the listing agreement, discuss other issues as well. For example, if there are certain times when you want the house off-limits for walk-throughs, let the agent know.

Also, consider negotiating the commission. If your house is expensive, an agent might not flinch if you suggest 4 or 5 percent instead of the usual 6. Conversely, if you know it's a buyer's market, consider offering the incentive of a higher commission if the agent can land you a sale within 5 percent of your asking price.

After you've signed a listing agreement, you may want to give your lawyer a call to notify him that you're selling your house and will need help reviewing bids and contracts. If you don't want to pay for a lawyer, your agent should also be able to guide you through this process but in some areas it's not possible or recommended to try to close on a home sale or purchase without a lawyer.

Getting Ready for an Open House

Whether you sell on your own or work with an agent, you'll want to spruce up your house before it goes on the market.

Take an objective look at it: Is it cluttered? A little worn and tired? Consider a new paint job. Tidy up. Move unneeded furniture into the attic, basement, or rented storage. Remove some of your personal items, like family pictures and knickknacks. Mow the lawn. Plant flowers, if it's the right season. These seemingly insignificant details can add many thousands of dollars to your eventual sales price.

If you're no good at this kind of thing, consider hiring a home stager, someone with experience preparing homes for showings. Their fees can be more than offset by quicker sales and higher selling prices. There are also good books and magazine articles on staging a home for sale.

Speaking of which, you'll need to settle on an asking price. When it comes to pricing your property, the only yardstick that matters is what comparable homes are selling for in your neighborhood now—which may be more, or less, than you sank into it. As with stocks, the market simply doesn't care what you paid for the house.

Your research will already have given you a good idea of how the market is faring. Your agent should also provide you with

How to Speak Money—*Talking Points*

Christine says

If the most important thing for you is getting your kid in a good school, then don't buy where the schools aren't good. Instead, rent where the good schools are. To me, an investment in your child's education is, in this housing market, more important than an investment in a home.

comparable sales and discuss why your house should be priced higher or lower.

When Is the Best Time to Buy?

For those who want to buy but who want to wait until the market bottoms out, a word of caution: It's hard to identify the absolute right moment until after it's gone. But if right now isn't the perfect moment, it's undoubtedly a good one: Prices and interest rates are, as previously noted, extremely low.

Let's take a look at current conditions. In the first quarter of 2011, home prices dropped for the third quarter in a row. Nationally, we're at mid-2002 levels. Meanwhile, at the end of March, the monthly index that tracks 20 large metro areas dipped below its previous low of April 2009, essentially confirming a double-dip in home prices for much of the country.

What matters, though, isn't what house prices have done in the recent past; it's what they'll do in the future. And despite all the gloom and doom, history teaches us that it's reasonable to expect that, in most markets, prices will eventually stabilize and begin climbing again.

Why? For one thing, even though this housing bust has made many people rethink the once widely (and erroneously) held notion that real estate prices are immune to major setbacks, it's not as if consumers no longer aspire to own a home. When current renters were asked whether they would prefer to rent or buy in the future, 81 percent said they would like to buy a house at some point. This is strong evidence that a fundamental demand for housing exists.

Granted, it may take a while for this underlying demand to nudge prices upward, considering the weak jobs climate, the over-hang of housing inventory and the fear shared by many people that home prices could go even lower. But as house prices fall and buyers enter the market, sellers will be able to ask for more. That's the way markets work. If you'd like an example of how that dynamic has operated historically, take a look at Los Angeles.

After a big run-up in the 1980s, house prices in Los Angeles peaked in early 1990—and then dropped 27 percent over the next six years. But after hitting a trough in 1996, prices began to climb, and by the beginning of 2000 had risen 37 percent and regained their former peak.

How to Speak Money—*Talking Points*

Christine says

Be prepared to negotiate. Negotiate with your real estate agent, the home inspector—negotiate with everybody, because the market is weak. People are hungry for business and you're in the driver's seat.

We all know what happened next. Prices more than doubled over the following six years as Americans (abetted by all-too-eager lenders) went on a housing feeding frenzy that culminated in a bust. That's where we are now.

But the point is that even after sharp declines, housing markets can recover (assuming an area's underlying economy is sound), and prices do resume their upward trend. So it seems that this is a pretty good time to be looking for a house. Because not only are prices low, interest rates are, too.

Is it possible that prices might go lower still from here? Yes. But it's unrealistic to expect to call the bottom of the market and time your purchase just right. What you can do, though, is take advantage of the depressed market to do an extensive search for a house you like—and then use the leverage of a weak market to negotiate hard on price.

As a buyer, you're in the advantageous position of having time and market conditions on your side. Before you do anything, though, you need to make sure you've got realistic expectations.

There's an increasing sense that a house is first a place to live and then an investment, not the other way around. After a period where people became serial house flippers, there's also a growing awareness that owning a house is a long-term commitment.

In years past, the rule of thumb was that you should consider buying only if you planned on living in an area at least five years. Today, we'd advise even longer-term thinking: You probably shouldn't buy a house unless you plan to stay in it 7 to 10 years.

That's not to say you might not come out ahead for shorter periods, especially if you don't buy at the height of a bubble. But given the large transaction costs of buying and selling and a more subdued appreciation outlook, we'd err on the side of planning for a longer stay than a shorter one. Remember you have to amortize those transaction costs over the length of time you're going to stay in the house.

So take your time, give it the serious thought it deserves, and then—if you plan to be in it for the long haul—move forward.

How to Speak Money's Words to the Wise

1. Housing (*how'•zing*): We all have to live somewhere; most of us already do. It's when we're looking for a new place that the issue of renting versus buying becomes important. The key determinants of the solution that's best for you are: how much can you afford to put down; how much can you afford in carrying costs; and how long do you expect to stay in the dwelling.
2. Mortgage (*mohr"•ghij*): The document that lets you live in the house you're buying while you're paying for it. How much you pay for your mortgage is a function of prevailing interest rates and your own creditworthiness.
3. Agent (*ae'•jent*): All real estate, like politics, is local. That's among the reasons a professional real estate agent who knows the ins and outs of a given market can help you, whether you're buying or selling. In our view, the financial outlay is too great, and the ramifications of a mistake too serious, to attempt to purchase or sell on your own.

CHAPTER 11

Speaking Money on Budget

Most people find that budgets are a necessary evil. They're no fun, but they're the only practical way we can get a grip on our spending—and make sure that our money is being used the way we want it to be used.

A budget is a plan. You figure out what's coming in and what's going out and you address that reality. Identify your biggest expenses and identify your sources of income. Figure out how you can minimize your biggest expenses and augment your income. Maybe you can do one of those things; maybe you can do both of those things. Maybe you can't do either. But you have to figure it out before you can repair your personal balance sheet.

Most people don't know how much money they have. They learn they're out of money when the ATM tells them they've just overdrawn their account. At that point, they realize they're in a little bit of trouble. Don't let "most people" be you. If you're serious about moving forward and building a future, you're going to need more discipline than that.

Even if you're in the happy situation of having plenty of income, the homework involved in drawing up a budget can be instructive, since you may find that you are spending more than you wish on items like DVDs, electronic gadgetry, or restaurant meals.

Drawing up a budget is usually a combination of drudgery and embarrassment. Drudgery because it takes a long time to categorize everything; embarrassment because you can't help but confront your foolish spending decisions, such as that luxury sound system neither you nor your spouse listens to. One of the chief impediments to budgeting, in fact, is that most people would rather not know how they really use their money.

But don't worry. Any spending mistakes you're making are probably common and not impossible to kick. Moreover, the bulk of budgeting's pains are at the beginning.

After you have a budget in place—and you've fine-tuned it with a couple of months of actual spending—tracking your expenditures becomes almost automatic.

Setting up a budget generally requires three steps:

1. Identify how you're spending money now.
2. Evaluate your current spending and set goals that take into account your long-term financial objectives.
3. Track your spending to make sure it stays within those guidelines.

There are really only three ways to solve whatever financial problem you may have: You can make more money, spend less money, or do both.

So you have to figure out what the problem is and which combination of those solutions is going to work for you. In today's economy you can't just go out and get a second job, as you could in the 1990s. Back then, if you spent too much, you could get a part-time job and pay off that credit card. It's not so easy now.

If you need a job, you may have to create it for yourself, by determining what you're good at and identifying how you can make money at it. Or you're going to have to spend your time figuring out how to move up in the job you have.

 How to Speak Money—*Talking Points*

Christine says
Figure out what's coming in and what's going out and understand your reality. Identify your biggest expenses, identify your source of income, figure out how you can minimize your biggest expenses and augment your source of income. Maybe you could do one of those things. Maybe you can do both of those things. Maybe you could do neither. But you have to figure it out.

Chances are, if you're at DEFCON 5, as they said in *War Games*, you've already cut all your unnecessary spending. You've chopped it to the bone. That's when you have to go and figure out how to increase the revenue side of the balance sheet.

While a budget can be complicated, you can use software to save grief. Personal finance programs such as Quicken or Microsoft Money have built-in budget-making tools that can create your budget for you.

Software Makes Budgeting Easier

In Quicken, for example, every time you make a deposit, write a check, pay a credit card bill, or dispatch an electronic payment you are asked to assign it to a particular category such as *salary, clothing, groceries, child care,* or *health insurance.*

The drawback, of course, is that entering and categorizing all of your income and outflow is a tedious chore.

You can reduce the tedium by judiciously selecting categories. If you're only worried about tracking your recreation and leisure spending, for example, you could create categories that cover only those types of expenses. Everything else can accumulate under *miscellaneous revenue* or *miscellaneous expense.*

An even better solution is to track expenses using electronic banking. That way, you can download your payments and deposits directly from the bank, rather than having to enter them by hand. You'll still have to add the categories yourself.

Once you've got your spending tracked by category, drawing up a report requires only a few clicks of the mouse. Even better, such programs often have an automatic budget-creation feature that scans your spending in the past to help you estimate how much you'll spend going forward.

If your finances aren't wired, you can still get a good handle on your spending the old-fashioned way. Start by getting all your records together from the past 12 months, including pay stubs, loan proceeds, withdrawal slips, canceled checks, and itemized credit card statements. Then go through them and compile totals for your income and expenses in a set of categories that makes sense for you.

At the end of this exercise, you may still have a sizable lump of undocumented spending—typically, the money you withdraw in cash for your day-to-day needs. If this portion of your budget seems to be getting out of hand, keep a journal for the next four weeks in which you record every nickel you spend. You can use those results to extrapolate how your cash is being spent throughout the year.

Here Comes the Rain

Now that you've got a good picture of where your money is going, you can proceed to evaluate which parts of that spending should be raised or lowered.

This is especially urgent if you spend more than you make—a scary situation, for sure, but not an uncommon one. In fact, U.S. Department of Labor numbers show that many families making $50,000 or less are spending at least a few percentage points more money each year than they actually bring in.

Today, half of all Americans would struggle to come up with $2,000 for an unanticipated car repair, a large medical bill, or legal expenses.

In a recent study by the National Bureau of Economic Research, 28 percent of Americans said they "certainly" couldn't come up with $2,000 within 30 days, and another 22 percent said they "probably" wouldn't be able to do it, either.

Only a quarter of the population was sure they could get their hands on $2,000 in a pinch. That doesn't speak highly of our ability to set financial priorities, develop plans, or stick to budgets.

That doesn't mean that those people, or you, are headed for bankruptcy. But it does show that Americans are in the habit of borrowing to cover both short-term expenses, like those on credit cards, and long-term ones, such as buying cars and homes.

Granted, the past few years have been difficult ones. The recession hurt everyone. Over the 12 months preceding the writing of this chapter, 19 percent of Americans—almost one in five—dipped into retirement savings to cover expenses. We don't have to tell you that this is a financial sin. You should never borrow from savings to fund operating expenses.

A budget tells us what we can't afford, but it doesn't keep us from buying it.

—*William Feather, American author and publisher*

As of April 2011, only 18 percent of the public felt they were more comfortable with the amount of debt they were carrying then they were a year earlier. Just writing this paragraph makes us wince.

You have to understand that the most important part of speaking money is *doing* it. And the more you do it, the more comfortable you'll become taking responsibility for your finances, and the easier and more natural it will feel. You build your future one step at a time, and you take a step—or more—every day.

Let's just say that if your spending exceeds your income, then your top priority in constructing a budget should be to slash your spending, pronto.

What Does It Cost to Live?

How much of your income should you spend on living? We believe in a 70–10–10–10 budget distribution: 70 percent for your living expenses, 10 percent for savings, 10 percent to invest, and 10 percent for charity. That's the ideal, anyway. If you can't manage that, then—at a minimum—aim to spend no more than 90 percent of your income. That way, you'll have the other 10 percent left to save for your big-picture items.

A few words of advice here:

- Beware of luxuries dressed up as necessities. You know what they are. They're those items you hate to give up but that you can certainly live without. If your income doesn't cover your costs, then some of your spending is probably for luxuries— even if you haven't been thinking about them in that way.
- Watch out for cash leakage—it can derail even the best budget. If you find yourself returning to the ATM more than once a week or so, you need to start keeping better records to find out where that cash is going.
- When projecting your likely income for the year, don't include dollars that you can't be sure you'll receive, such as year-end bonuses, tax refunds, or investment gains. They're nice if they happen, but you should plan as though they won't.
- Watch out for spending creep. As raises, promotions, and investments start boosting your annual income, don't start spending for luxuries until you're sure that you're staying

ahead of inflation. It's better to use your extra income to pump more into your overall savings.

Once you've set your budget goals, it's likely that you'll find some of them are unrealistic. If so, ease them slightly. No point in giving yourself an unreachable hurdle, but neither should it be too easy. Often it takes two or three revisions before you achieve a budget that you can really stick to.

The most common spending problems are caused by a house that's too large, a car that's too luxurious, or a credit card lifestyle that's too lavish for your income. Those who see a virtue in moderation may have had budgeting in mind.

Whatever your situation, here are some common ways that people can reduce monthly bills.

- *Eliminate trivial but needless costs:* Look first for small savings. They won't end your budget problems, but they're easy to find and take advantage of. Maybe it's that mid-afternoon Danish or expensive premium latte. Look for clothes and household furnishings only during sales. Bundle your various shopping trips to save on gas. Keep your house warmer in summer and cooler in winter. Take on chores that you currently pay someone else to perform, such as mowing the lawn or shoveling snow. None of these savings will make much

How to Speak Money—*Talking Points*

Ali says

When it comes to speaking money, you have got to commit to learning the hard words, and you've got to become comfortable using the hard words. It doesn't actually matter if you know all the peripheral adjectives. If you don't know the hard words and how to use them, you're not going to speak money.

It's like losing weight: You've either got to diet or you've got to exercise, but you can't just think about it and expect results. We treat money like we treat those "as-seen-on-TV" exercise things, where you don't have to do any work—you can just basically stare at this thing and you'll lose weight. Money is going to take some work.

difference by themselves, but put them together and they do add up.
- *Reduce larger expenses:* These recommendations are decidedly more painful. If you smoke, for example, take steps to quit. Don't buy season tickets to anything. Trade in your luxury car or sport utility vehicle for something a lot cheaper to buy, fuel, and maintain (we did say this was painful).

On the assumption that those kinds of changes may be too wrenching, here are some other specific areas where many people can find savings:

- *Refinance your mortgage:* If new mortgages are costing at least two percentage points less than the rate you're paying, refinancing may save you significant dollars. Mortgage rates in late 2011 fell below 5 percent. We may never see these rates again.
- *Cut your taxes:* Usually this means taking better advantage of itemized deductions, which is a lot easier to do if you're either self-employed or have some income from work you do outside of a regular job. That opens up a range of new deductions—from expenses for work-related items to a home office—that are much harder to claim if you're an ordinary working stiff.

   On the investment side, you can save some money by selling, and then writing off, investments that have lost money. You can use such losses to offset any gains you may have in a given year. If your losses outweigh your gains, you can deduct as much as $3,000 of investment losses from your ordinary income each year. Those with higher incomes may also be able to save some money by shifting money out of taxable bonds into tax-free municipal bonds.
- *Appeal your home assessment:* If you're a home owner, you may even be able to cut your real estate taxes by challenging the value that the local assessor puts on your property. You have to have good evidence, of course. You should call the assessor's office first to make sure you understand the formula for determining the house's value (the assessment listed on tax bills is often only a fraction of the real value that determines your tax).

If recent home sales in your neighborhood lead you to believe that your house is worth less than its assessment and a qualified real estate agent writes an appraisal in support of your claim, then you can file a grievance with the assessor's office and possibly get your bill reduced. The cost: $200 to $300 for the written appraisal. If an attorney handles the appeal for you, he will typically charge 50 percent of the first year's tax savings. We think every homeowner in a high-tax state should be doing this.

The preceding suggestions won't work for everyone, and you may have considered them already. But since you alone are privy to the numbers in your budget, you alone know how radically you need to cut. If our suggestions don't appeal, find your own alternatives.

Getting Out of Debt

You might think that from what we've just discussed, we'd be telling you to avoid debt at all costs. But the truth is that debt can be a good thing. Take a mortgage, for example—it allows you to live in your home even though you can't afford to pay for it all at once. Or consider student loans. They let you get an education that is likely to lead to a more financially rewarding career than you could otherwise obtain. When amortized over the length of your working life, the money you borrowed to pay for college is likely to be one of the best investments you ever made.

So when it comes to debt, we're not in favor of total abstinence. We're in favor of sensible, practical borrowing for particular situations, consistent with your goals and your finances.

Before you decide to borrow, ask yourself these questions:

- Why are you taking on the debt?
- Is it for something you truly need or will it make your life significantly better?
- Can you get what you want without the debt or without inflicting undue hardship on you and your family?
- Will borrowing restrict your ability to maneuver financially in the future?
- How much debt can you handle without jeopardizing your financial security?

If you give these questions serious thought, you'll be able to tell when it pays to borrow and when it doesn't.

If you decide to borrow so you can own a home, fine. But that doesn't mean you should buy more house than you can afford by taking on more debt than you can manage. Nor should you opt for a mortgage with a teaser rate that could bust your budget when the rate resets.

The same goes for a car. Borrowing to buy a car that makes it easier to commute to work is reasonable. Buying a decked-out mobile home with a loan so huge that the crushing payments force you to forego or skimp on 401(k) contributions—well, that's a different story.

Of course, in reality, people find all sorts of ways to rationalize questionable borrowing. Sometimes they confuse *need* with *want*. We may want that new 70-inch LED LCD TV. But that doesn't mean we really need it.

Or they justify borrowing on investment grounds. A few years ago when it seemed home prices were going only up, many people borrowed against their home equity so they could invest the loan proceeds. There's a name for this practice. It's called *gambling*.

Sometimes deals seem so good that people don't even realize they're headed for trouble. That's often the case with credit cards, with which a combination of easy borrowing, teaser rates, and low minimum payments makes it shockingly easy for people to suddenly find themselves in deep water.

Still, that doesn't mean that we should avoid all debt at all times. A more rational response is to be prudent about evaluating when to take on debt.

The one time when people should seriously consider ridding themselves of debt is when they're in or entering retirement.

Without a regular paycheck, without the opportunity for income to grow, it's much harder to manage debt—and it's easier to get overwhelmed by it. But even in retirement there may be times when debt could be helpful. If someone is struggling but has substantial home equity, for example, a reverse mortgage may be a way to improve one's standard of living.

So here's an area where we agree: We both recommend taking a nuanced view that recognizes that debt can be good, bad, or something in between, depending on the situation and how carefully you handle it.

How to Speak Money's Words to the Wise

1. Debt (*det*): On the plus side, debt allows us to benefit from items we don't yet fully own, from our homes to our cars, to—on occasion—stocks and bonds. Concepts such as borrowing, lending, credit, interest payments, and the like provide us with the means to improve our lives before we could otherwise do so. On the other hand, some people become addicted to debt and accumulate much more than they can repay. They forfeit their ability to build a future as they become seduced by the *now*. Debt is a complex and nuanced topic, and it deserves your careful study.

2. Budget (*buh'•jit*): The easiest way to control your spending and map your future. Everybody says they want complete freedom, but it's not really true. Most of us, in some aspects of our lives, would prefer to be told what to do. When you develop a budget, you're telling yourself what to do: the best of both worlds. Following a plan and tracking achievements strokes the side of us that enjoys order and secure progress. And, budgets really work.

3. Software (*saw'•fwair*): It's so much easier to set up and track a budget than it used to be. Software programs—Moneydance, Quicken, and YNAB, among others—offer easy-to-use features that make budgeting simple and, at the same time, provide highly detailed information. Many of these programs have apps that work on smartphones and iPads.

12

Speaking Money in Retirement

A long and happy retirement is supposed to be the reward for a life well lived. It's the proof that you've conducted yourself appropriately through your working years. You've been prudent, looking toward the future, saving and investing so that, at the end of the day, you'll be able to travel, learn Greek, devote your time to woodworking, volunteer with underprivileged children, or simply relax without the financial worries that would make such activities impossible.

That's the dream, anyway. But for far too many of us, it remains just that—a dream.

It's a bit simplistic, but not necessarily inaccurate, to suggest that the world is divided into two kinds of people: ants and grasshoppers. We all remember the fable, right? The industrious ant gathered grain all summer, toiling and saving to prepare for the cold, harsh winter ahead. The grasshopper, meanwhile, fiddled away. He traveled expensively, threw his money around and bought fancy clothes, bling, and the latest electronic gadgets.

When winter came, the ant had food and a warm house. The grasshopper was huddled in a men's shelter, emerging only to panhandle, trying to get by on a smile and a shoeshine. He'd pawned his bling, his electronics were obsolete, and his dated clothes barely covered his thorax.

If you're one of the ants of this world, you've already mastered the most important element of retirement planning: discipline. You may need some help in understanding which investment vehicles are most appropriate for you, or exactly how much you should be putting away each month so that you'll be sure to reach your goals, but at least you *have* goals and you're working toward them.

If, on the other hand, you're one of life's grasshoppers—and there are many, many, many of them—then the path is a bit more difficult. Because it involves a change in mind-set. It requires you to look at life objectively, renounce magical thinking—the idea that somehow things will work out—and develop a detailed plan for the future and stick to it. This may be something you've never done. It may even be something that you think you can't do. But you can. And you must. Because, as hard as it may be for you to turn yourself into someone who can build a responsible future, it will be infinitely more difficult to live without money. And the longer you live, the more unpleasant your circumstances will become.

The Historical Perspective

In the south of France, the town of Arles is now a quaint artist and tourist destination, but it was originally founded as a retirement village for Roman soldiers. Survive past age 40, and the emperor would give you a house, some land to farm, and up to 17 years pay to live off of. It was a rather extreme way to save for retirement—expanding the empire at the tip of a sword—but if you weren't a Roman soldier, there was no such thing as retirement. Retirement? What retirement? For thousands of years, just about everyone simply worked until they died.

The man who invented modern retirement was Chancellor Otto von Bismarck of Germany. In 1883, he promised to pay a pension to all nonworking Germans over the age of 65. Despite the fact that hardly anyone lived to age 65—there were no antibiotics and life was hard—his offer appeased countrymen who might otherwise have gone Marxist, which was a potential problem at the time. So Bismarck, without necessarily intending to, set an arbitrary age for retirement that became the Western standard, and he also established the idea that the government should pay people for being old.

Skip ahead a couple of decades and we have the world-renowned physician, William Osler, providing a rationale for retirement. In 1905, he gave a speech at Johns Hopkins Hospital, where he'd been physician-in-chief, and announced that evidence suggested that workers over 60 were, in his words, "useless." He'd studied the matter, he said. Workers between 25 and 40 were in their "15 golden years of plenty." Then there was a distinct fall-off in quality over the next 20 years, and after that, well. . . .

Retirement came in very handy in the United States, where lots of old people caused great unemployment among younger workers by refusing to leave their jobs. The Great Depression made the situation even worse. As Mary-Lou Weisman noted in the *New York Times* article titled "The History of Retirement: From Early Man to A.A.R.P.," "It was a Darwinian sacrificial moment. Retirement was a necessary adaptation and everybody knew it, but the old guys were not going quietly. The toughest among them refused to quit, even when plant managers turned up the conveyor belts to Chaplinesque speeds."

She continued:

> By 1935, it became evident that the only way to get old people to stop working for pay was to pay them enough to stop working. A Californian, Francis Townsend, initiated a popular movement by proposing mandatory retirement at age 60. In exchange, the Government would pay pensions of up to $200 a month, an amount equivalent at the time to a full salary for a middle-income worker. Horrified at the prospect of Townsend's radical generosity, President Franklin D. Roosevelt proposed the Social Security Act of 1935, which made workers pay for their own old-age insurance.

But if people were not going to work, what were they going to do? Most retired people longed for work. In general, most Americans don't have the capacity to enjoy doing nothing.

So leisure years were invented. Again, from Weisman in *The New York Times*:

> Retirement communities, where older people did not have to see younger people working, began to appear in the 1920s and 30s. The number of golf courses in the United States tripled between 1921 and 1930. Subsequent technological developments like movies and television helped turn having nothing to do into a leisure time activity. From now on, the elderly would work at play.

How to Speak Money—*Talking Points*

Ali says

We have an unrealistic expectation of retirement. It's based on a manufacturing workforce, where you have backbreaking horrible labor for all these years, and then you need to rest, and you need to get some money for resting. I'm not sure that's the case anymore.

I think younger people need to think about retirement as something different. We need to change our expectations. We need to think of retirement as opportunity. I think of retirement as the opportunity to do things that I haven't done before. For example, I don't think I ever got enough education. So I would love to do that.

As lives have gotten longer, retirement has grown to become a bigger chunk of time. The average U.S. life expectancy is now almost 78 years, and the older you get, the older you are likely to get. The challenge today isn't so much to reach retirement age; it's to make sure you don't outlive your money.

Retirement Is Expensive

We see study after study of people who underestimate what their retirement costs are going to be. You really have to understand your potential health care costs and how long you might live. You really have to come to grips with how your money is going to grow.

To do that, you have to know what your money is for. In the preretirement world, people save money for a trip, for a house, or for education. It's the same in retirement. You're going to want to travel. You're going to need a car. You're going to need health care and insurance. You need to plan for each of those individual buckets.

Retirement is not one golden amorphous end, bathed in pastels with soft-focus edges. It's real. It's a series of day-to-day decisions, actions, and purchases. You must plan, save, and prepare for each of them.

The recent recession was difficult for everyone. But it was particularly cruel to retirees and those close to retirement, those with little time left to rebuild their savings.

One in four Americans age 50 or older said they had exhausted all of their savings during the recession, while 67 percent had reduced their retirement savings account balances at least somewhat during the previous three years, according to a recent report by the AARP Public Policy Institute.

The question isn't at what age I want to retire; it's at what income.

—*George Foreman, businessman, former boxing champion*

More than half, 53 percent, said they were not confident that they would have enough money to live comfortably in retirement.

"Many older Americans have been buffeted by skyrocketing health care costs, dwindling home values, shrinking pension and investment portfolios, and employment struggles," John Rother, AARP's executive vice president for policy, strategy, and international affairs, said in a statement.

More than 80 percent said the economy had affected their retirement plans. During the recession, nearly one-third said their home declined substantially in value and one-quarter experienced a job loss.

Of those who reported struggling to make ends meet, 12 percent opted to forgo their health insurance in the previous three years, and 50 percent put off medical or dental care or were not taking their medication because of financial considerations.

"Older Americans have good reason to be worried about the future because they have less time than others to recover from the impact of the last three years," Rother said. "When older Americans

The Keys to Retirement Planning

Christine
1. Start early
2. Be aggressive
3. Save for retirement first

Ali
1. Don't underestimate your costs
2. Know what your money is for
3. Have buckets for everything

are borrowing against their future or betting against their health, serious challenges lie ahead."

The year 2011 marks a significant milestone for the Baby Boomer generation. It's when the first of them turn 65 and begin to retire. Baby Boomers, born between 1946 and 1964, number 77 million and represent about 37 percent of the nation's total population age 16 or older, according to government statistics.

"Boomers have been scarred by the economic turmoil of the past few years and face complex challenges going forward," said Clark M. Blackman II, chair of the Personal Financial Planning Executive Committee at the American Institute of Certified Public Accountants. "While more optimistic about the markets, many Boomers remain uncertain about the U.S. economy and their own situations as they contend with job loss—their own and their children's—lower home values and rising education costs."

How can you avoid being one of those unfortunate statistics? How can you realistically fund a satisfying retirement? The rules are simple: Start early. Be aggressive. Put your retirement money away and look away so you can let it grow. Know your risk tolerance and know what you want your money to do for you. And—and this is the most important one—*always save for retirement first, no matter what decision you're making with your money.*

Consider this conversation, overheard in the hallways here at CNN: "Oh, I have to put a new fence around my backyard. I'm going to have to stop contributing to my 401(k) for four or five months to get that done." We almost knocked her over to stop her and say, "No, no, no! Don't do it! That fence is not going to buy your food when you're 82 years old."

If you stop contributing to your 401(k) because you're using that money to buy something that's not critically essential, you're making a terrible mistake. Your kid can always borrow for college. You cannot borrow for your retirement. So retirement must come first.

Programs to Fund Your Retirement

Fortunately, the government helps you save for retirement in several ways. Retirement plans, such as IRAs and 401(k) plans, allow your investments to grow tax deferred. That means you don't pay

How to Speak Money—*Talking Points*

Christine says

My very first boss said to me, "Here, sit down. I'm going to show you how to log in to the company 401(k) and I'm going to get you signed up." He put me in for the maximum contribution. I was 21 years old. I didn't care. He said, "You have to do it now so you don't know you'll miss it." He was absolutely right.

So earlier this year, it was my turn. I took a young, new producer and I said, "You know what? Let's get you signed up for the company 401(k). We'll have you contribute the maximum. You won't even know you'll miss it, I promise you."

When she said, "I don't make very much money," I said, "That's the point. You have no kids, no mortgage, no car payment. You're not going to miss it."

You have to convince yourself you're not going to miss it, and you have to live a little below your means so that you have a bit of extra money to put away for other savings programs. The best time to be planning your retirement is at least 10 years before you even have a gray hair! Time is more important than money in retirement planning. The best thing you can do is sit a young person down and make them save. I am so grateful my first boss did.

income tax on the money you invest, or on the growth of that money while it's in the account. You can keep all the profits you make on your retirement plan assets, and reinvest those profits to get the benefits of compounding, for as long as that money is kept in the plan. And if that's not enough of an incentive, many companies match a percentage of your 401(k) contribution to encourage saving.

You can read more about voluntary defined contribution plans such as 401(k)s, 403(b)s, and IRAs by clicking on CNNMoney's excellent retirement guide at: money.cnn.com/retirement/guide/401kandCos.

When you reach retirement age and begin withdrawing your plan assets, you'll have to pay income taxes on the withdrawals, but thanks to the compound interest you've earned, you're still way ahead. The government doesn't give us that many great deals; let's take advantage of the opportunities when they're here.

401(k) Plans

Contributing money to a 401(k) gives you an immediate tax-deductible, tax-deferred growth on your savings, and—usually—a matching contribution from your company. That matching contribution is about as close to a free lunch as there is, so eat up.

Today, workers 50 and older may contribute an additional amount—$5,000 as of when this chapter was written—above the maximum allowable 401(k) contribution. It's a great way to make up for lost time.

Of course, while federal law sets the guidelines for 401(k) plans, your employer may set tighter restrictions. Plus, it may take time for the administrators of your plan to implement the changes.

For all its tax advantages, the 401(k) is not a penalty-free ride. Pull out money from your account before age 59½, and with few exceptions, you'll owe income taxes on the amount withdrawn plus an additional 10 percent penalty.

Also, be aware of your plan's vesting schedule—that's the time you're required to work at the company before you're allowed to walk away with 100 percent of your employer matches. Of course, any money you contribute to a 401(k) is yours.

Individual Retirement Account (IRA)

An IRA is another excellent long-term option for you. Like a 401(k), IRAs offer huge tax breaks. Even if you have a 401(k) or other tax-advantaged savings plan at work, you should consider investing in an IRA to augment your retirement savings plan.

There are two types of IRAs: a traditional IRA and a Roth IRA. A traditional IRA grows tax-deferred, meaning you pay taxes on your investment gains only when you make withdrawals. By contrast, you put your money into a Roth IRA after you've paid taxes on it, but it offers tax-free growth, meaning you owe no tax when you make withdrawals. With a little study, you can determine which is best for you.

You may be able to deduct some or all of your contributions to a traditional IRA. You may also be eligible for a tax credit equal to a percentage of your contribution. IRAs cannot be owned jointly. However, any amounts remaining in your IRA upon your death can be paid to your beneficiary or beneficiaries.

To contribute to a traditional IRA, you must be under age 70½ by the end of the tax year. You or your spouse, or both of you if you file a joint return, must have taxable compensation, such as wages, salaries, commissions, tips, bonuses, or net income from self-employment. Taxable alimony and separate maintenance payments received by an individual are treated as compensation for IRA purposes.

Play a Waiting Game

But what if you are one of those individuals who, because of factors beyond your control, find yourself approaching your retirement years without the financial cushion you'd hoped for? Then, to put it simply, work as long as you can and delay collecting Social Security. The longer you wait, the more money you'll draw when you retire.

For Baby Boomers born between 1943 and 1954 (yes, 1943 is before the Baby Boom era officially began, but the government includes those pre-Boomers in the 1983 amendments to the Social Security law), the full retirement age is now 66, but they're eligible to begin collecting Social Security payments at age 62. For every year a Boomer waits until age 70, though, the more he will receive in the monthly check. Of course, anything involving money—and mortality—isn't simple. Your choice will depend on your health, your job status, and what you have in various bank, pension, and 401(k) accounts.

Each of these elements will influence when you decide to begin collecting the money that the government has been keeping for you. And remember, it's *your* money. You've paid it into the trust fund, the government's invested it for you over the years, and now you're getting it back.

You may not be in a position to postpone those initial Social Security payments when you turn 62. You may not have sufficient resources to enable you to live any other way. If that's the case, you're not alone. As we'll see, there are millions of Baby Boomers in that boat with you.

But if you can delay somehow, you should. Because the numbers, worked out by the AARP, are clear.

Let's say that at 62, you're getting a check for $1,000 a month. If you can hold off for five more years, until you're 67, then based on that number, you can get $500 more each month. That's a 50 percent jump.

And if you can wait until you're 70, you can gain almost $900 more each month. Every year you wait, you get an 8 percent increase in monthly benefits.

And there's an extra plus for married couples: The younger spouse can collect on an older spouse's benefits and delay collecting their own benefits until age 70. The couple, literally, reaps the benefits of waiting.

Now, we want to be very clear that Social Security won't pay for everything you need in retirement. But the longer you wait, the more your monthly expenses are covered by your Social Security check. If you wait until age 70, according to AARP, Social Security will cover 82 percent of your living expenses.

Start collecting at 62, by contrast, and just 36 percent of living expenses are covered. So those eight years make a dramatic difference. Not everyone, of course, can afford to wait until age 70. But if you are in good health and can put off collecting for even a year or two, it works in your favor.

And if you want to calculate for yourself, both the Social Security Administration and the AARP websites have calculators. You can plug in the numbers and see what you'll end up with.

Remember, too, that the Social Security Administration (SSA) works on a 35-year maximum. So let's say you made $150,000 after working 30 years, but in your thirty-fifth year of working you're making $200,000: The SSA will compute your payment based on the higher number, so you get the maximum benefits.

And if you think that you can simply keep working at your present job to earn the income you need after you turn 65, think again. One of the most striking changes in the American labor market during the twentieth century was the virtual disappearance of older men from the workforce.

 Financial Benefits of Postponing the Collection of Social Security

(Assumes payment of $1,000 each month at age 62)

Age 62–$1,000 each month
Age 67–$500 more each month
Age 70–$900 more each month
Age 62–36 percent of living expenses covered
Age 70–82 percent of living expenses covered

Source: AARP.

For some people the obvious—if disappointing solution—to not having saved enough money for retirement is simply to work longer, for more years. But, depending on who you are, and what you do, this simply may not be an option for you. As the makeup of the workforce continues to change workers—men in particular—have less control over WHEN they retire, regardless of their health or energy level.

In 1880, 78 percent of men aged 65 and older were part of the labor force. By 1990, that figure had declined to less than 20 percent. In recent decades, the labor force participation rate of men 55 to 64 has been declining as well. So there's no guarantee you'll be able to keep your job, even if you continue to do it well.

Again, back in agrarian days, before there was any such thing as retirement planning, people had lots of children in part because they expected their kids to take care of them in their old age. Many wills from colonial New England, for example, include detailed clauses spelling out the care that children were to give the surviving parent. And when an elderly parent transferred property directly to a child, the contracts often specified the amount of food and firewood the child was to supply to the parent.

So it could be argued that people viewed children as a substitute strategy for retirement planning. Studies of the time show that as the number of children decreased, the savings rate went up. That might suggest that a couple had more money to put away when they had fewer children, or it might reflect the realization that, with kids abandoning the farm for the cities and the factories, an elderly couple couldn't depend on their children for care. It's probably a bit of both.

Social Security: The Nation's Safety Net

Given that just about everyone who holds a job has a Social Security card, it's surprising how many people don't really know much about the program. The following is a brief history.

The Social Security system was designed in 1935, during the Great Depression, to provide pension benefits to those not covered by a private pension plan. It was a time when the entire country was hurting, but the pain disproportionately affected the elderly who were unable to work and often had no means of support.

The Social Security Act consisted of two programs, Old Age Assistance (OAA) and Old Age Insurance (OAI). The OAA program provided federal matching funds to subsidize state old age pension programs.

With federal funds suddenly available to the states, many of them quickly developed a pension program or increased existing benefits. By 1950, 22 percent of the population ages 65 and over received benefits through OAA. The program peaked at this point, though. It soon fell behind the newly liberalized OAI, which began to dominate Social Security.

The OAI program is the one we're all familiar with. It's what we mean when we say, "Social Security." It's administered by the federal government and financed by payroll taxes. Retirees (and survivors of retirees, dependents of retirees, and the disabled) who have paid into the system are eligible to receive benefits. The program remained small until 1950, when coverage was extended to include farm and domestic workers, and average benefits were increased by 77 percent.

Jump ahead to 1965, and the Social Security Act was amended to include Medicare, which provides health insurance to the elderly. The Social Security program continued to expand in the late 1960s and early 1970s—benefits increased 13 percent in 1968, another 15 percent in 1969, and 20 percent in 1972.

But in the late 1970s and early 1980s Congress was finally forced to slow the growth of Social Security benefits, as the struggling economy led to the possibility that the program could go bankrupt. In 1977, the formula for determining benefits was adjusted downward. Reforms in 1983 included the delay of a cost-of-living adjustment, the taxation of up to half of benefits, and payroll tax increases.

Despite these changes, Social Security benefits today are still the main source of retirement income for most retirees.

Summing It Up

At the beginning of the twentieth century, life expectancy was 47 years. By 1935, when Social Security was created, it had expanded to 63 years. In general, people didn't live long enough to worry about supporting themselves for a prolonged period of old age. By the end of the twentieth century, though, life expectancy had increased to 77 years and it continues to rise. Today, 65 is the new 40 and, with the biotechnology revolution and improving health care, many people may spend as much time in retirement as they did in a job. That is a game-changing development.

While the response to the new reality of retirement has been varied, it's clear that retirement planning has entered a new phase. The old model was simple: Accumulate enough wealth during the first half of life so that you could spend it all in the second half of life. Life spans during retirement were short enough that one's savings goals, inflation risks, and other problems were manageable.

It's different now. It's possible to live 30 years or more in retirement, and that magnifies the impact of various risks. These include actuarial risks (outliving your savings), investment risk, and inflation risk. When retirement lasted 10 to 15 years, inflation and investment return were just inconvenient details, because you spent your savings proportionately over your expected remaining life.

But when we're talking about a time period of 30 years or more, dribbling away your principal is a form of financial suicide. What happens if you live 10 years longer than expected? What happens if inflation is 2 percent higher or your return on investment is 2 percent lower? It could mean financial catastrophe, because small percentage changes compounded over long periods of time cause huge changes in your retirement savings.

Many professional retirement planners are responding to these changes with more dynamic program models. These include traditional elements, such as savings, pension, Social Security, and health care, while supplementing them with features like defined contribution plans, second careers, and part-time income.

Living Your Golden Years

Maybe you're ready to think about one of the issues most important to retirement: where you'd like to be. How do you select your criteria? There are likely to be some very personal considerations, such as where your children and grandchildren are located. You may want a climate that allows you to play golf year round, or to be near a college where you can take courses.

Most of us have to live our working lives within striking distance of our places of employment. This may be less important in years to come, when telecommuting, teleconferencing, and tele-everything-else changes the way work is done. But for people old enough to be considering retirement seriously, the commute to the office, store, studio, or factory has been a constant for many years. In retirement, though, one has no such tether.

Money magazine recently published a list of the best places to retire to. They considered the availability of jobs; air and water quality; the general direction of housing prices; demographic makeup of the community; educational, recreational, and cultural opportunities; quality of medical care; climate; crime; and many more quality-of-life components.

It's interesting to see what's *not* on the list. There's no New York City, no Boston, and no Los Angeles. These locales would be at or near the top of anyone's choices for culture, for medical care, food, and educational opportunities. They're also among the most expensive locales in America. So *Money* isn't providing an inventory for jet setters; it's giving us a carefully researched look at hidden gems on the domestic landscape, with attractive climates, amenities, and cost and value ratios.

To see the list, simply go to http://money.cnn.com/magazines/moneymag/bplive/2010/.

The beautiful part of retirement is that, if you plan for it, it gives you the ability to be yourself once you've had a lifetime to figure out who you are.

How to Speak Money's Words to the Wise

1. Decades (*deh'•kaed'z*): We're living longer than ever, which means that retirement can often last for 20 years or more. By the time you're ready to retire, you may be living longer still. You need sufficient reserves so that you don't outlive your money. The longer you live, the more you'll need.

2. Today (*tu-dae'*): Start planning now. It's not that hard, but it is that important. Every dollar you put into your retirement savings can be worth a great deal more if you follow the basic investing rules we've discussed previously.

3. Expensive (*ek•spen'•siv*): The most common mistake made by people in retirement is underestimating their costs. It's ironic that what we call the *golden years* are often defined by an ever-shrinking standard of living. When you retire, what will really be different? You still have to eat; you still need a place to live; you'll probably need a car, want to travel, see the grandkids, and so on. The main difference is that you won't have a steady paycheck to pay for it all.

Afterword

We've had a terrific time writing this book. We hope you find reading it just as rewarding. We've tried to explain the most important trends reshaping our world, and to suggest the strategies you can employ to turn them to your advantage.

Some of what we've discussed is global and macro; other parts are specific and individual. That's the way speaking money works. It's an integrated language that runs like a bloodstream through the living world.

To those who might have expected more fighting between us, we apologize. Of course, we have our areas of disagreement, but when we examined the conditions facing us all, we found that we pretty much concurred on the broad stroke responses. In fact, the victory is that we found a great way to do this together. We're very pleased to be disappointed in the lack of conflict we've had.

We've learned from each other. We've learned how to understand each other, and we've learned to cherish and respect the differences that got us to where we are.

We hope you make the same discoveries as you learn to speak money. Because you'll find that speaking money can open the door to better communication in many, many areas of your life.

Bibliography

American Express OPEN. "The American Express OPEN State of Women-Owned Businesses Report." March, 2011.

Banjo, Shelly. "Seven Questions to Ask When Picking a Financial Advisor." *Wall Street Journal,* April 13, 2009.

Bernard, Tara Siegel. "Financial Advice by Women for Women." *New York Times,* April 23, 2010.

Boston Consulting Group. "Made in the USA, Again: Manufacturing Is Expected to Return to America as China's Rising Labor Costs Erase Most Savings." *Offshoring,* May 2011.

Damodaran, Aswath. "Historical Returns on Stocks, Bonds and Bills." New York University Stern School of Business. http://pages.stern.nyu.edu/~adamodar/New_Home_Page/datafile/histret.html#_msoanchor_1.

Dickler, Jessica. "How to find a job in 2011." *CNN Money,* May 18, 2011. http://money.cnn.com/2011/05/18/pf/jobs/how_to_find_a_job/index.htm.

Fisher, Anne. "Dads Under More Pressure at Work and at Home." *Fortune,* June 15, 2011. http://management.fortune.cnn.com/2011/06/15/dads-under-more-pressure-at-work-and-at-home/.

Greenstone, Michael and Adam Looney. "College Is Expensive, But Still a Smart Choice." *Brookings.edu,* August 15, 2011. www.brookings.edu/opinions/2011/0815_college_greenstone_looney.aspx.

Hamilton, James and Drew Liming. *Careers in Wind Energy.* Bureau of Labor Statistics, November 2010.

Hira, Tahira K and Cäzilia Loibl. "Gender differences in investment behavior: research and marketing implications." *NASD Investor Education Foundation,* August 31, 2007.

Hollander, Sophia. "Private School Tuition Bill Tops $40,000." *Wall Street Journal,* June 20, 2011.

Investopedia. "Bonds." www.investopedia.com/investing-topics/Bonds.

Investopedia. "Stocks." www.investopedia.com/investing-topics/Stocks.

Izzo, Phil. "Nearly 1 in 3 Unemployed Out of Work More Than a Year." *Wall Street Journal,* May 3, 2011.

Leonhardt, David. "Rent or Buy, a Matter of Lifestyle." *New York Times,* May 10, 2011.

Leonhardt, David. "Even for Cashiers, College Pays Off." *New York Times,* June 25, 2011.

Roy, Hampton, MD and Russell, Charles, PhD. *The Encyclopedia of Aging and the Elderly.* Iowa City, IA: MedRounds Publications, 1992, 2005.

Sellery, Bruce. *Moolala: Why Smart People Do Dumb Things with Their Money (and What You Can Do About It).* Toronto: McClelland & Stewart, Ltd., 2010.

Rooney, Ben. "Half of workers unhappy in their jobs." CNN Money, June 20, 2011. http://money.cnn.com/2011/06/20/news/economy/ workers_disgruntled/index.htm.

Short, Joanna. "Economic History of Retirement in the United States." EH.net, February 1, 2010. http://eh.net/encyclopedia/article/short .retirement.history.us.

Tresidder, Todd. *The History of Retirement Planning.* November 17, 2009. www.thehistoryof.net/history-retirement-planning.

Tseng, Nin-Hai. "A College Degree Returns More than the Stock Market." Fortune.com, June 30, 2011. http://finance.fortune.cnn.com/2011/06/ 30/a-college-degree-returns-more-than-the-stock-market/.

United States Central Intelligence Agency. *The 1990 CIA World Factbook,* www.gutenberg.org/ebooks/14.

United States Central Intelligence Agency. *The 2010 CIA World Factbook,* www.cia.gov/library/publications/the-world-factbook/index.html.

Wade, Nicholas. "Teeth of Human Ancestors Hold Clues to Their Family Life." *New York Times,* June 1, 2011.

Weisman, Mary Lou. "The History of Retirement, From Early Man to A.A.R.P." *New York Times,* March 21, 1999.

Workplace Options. "Demands of Changing Workforce Ramp Up Pressure on Working Dads." June 7, 2011. www.workplaceoptions.com/news/ press-releases/press-release.asp?id=F9FDCE88426C49F99605&title= Demands%20of%20Changing%20Workforce%20Ramp%20up%20 Pressure%20on%20Working%20Dads.

About the Authors

Ali and Christine met when they were both reporters and anchors for CNN*fn*, where they hosted various shows from the studio and from the floor of the New York Stock Exchange. Since then, they have jointly covered every major economic story of the last decade: the high-tech boom and bust, 9/11, the corporate scandals of 2001, the Enron trial, the mass auto-industry layoffs of the mid 2000s, the financial crisis of 2008, TARP, the 2008 election, the stimulus bill, and the debt debate. Their in-depth reporting for CNN's "How the Wheels Came Off" was honored with a National Headliner Award for Business & Consumer Reporting in 2010.

What's unique about Ali and Christine is that they have different perspectives on money, yet every day come together to translate for CNN viewers what complicated economics mean for their own family. Christine is a saver. Ali's a spender. Christine drives a minivan. Ali drives a motorcycle. Christine is cautious. Ali likes risk. Together, daily, they give their viewers, readers, and listeners the complete story on how to get the best return on your dollar, how to talk to your boss for a raise, whether it's the right time to buy a house, and whether interest rates will rise or fall.

Ali Velshi

As CNN's Chief Business Correspondent, when Ali's not in studio in New York, Ali's out reporting. In addition to logging thousands of miles across the country on the CNN Express bus, Velshi has reported live from hurricanes Katrina, Gustav, and Ike, the Gulf of Mexico oil spill, and from Pakistan after the assassination of Presidential Candidate Benazir Bhutto. He anchored CNN's breaking news coverage of the attempted terror attack on a flight into Detroit, for which CNN was nominated for a 2010 Emmy. He was also honored with a 2010 Alumni Achievement Award from his alma mater, Queen's University, from which he has a degree in Religion.

Velshi writes a monthly column for *Money* and for Delta *Sky*, and posts the weekly *Ali V Podcast* on iTunes. His first book, *Gimme My Money Back: Your Guide to Beating the Financial Crisis*, was published in 2009. Velshi played himself in the Oliver Stone film *Wall Street: Money Never Sleeps* and has cameos with Christine in *Sex and the City 2* and *Too Big to Fail*. He hopes this book will land him more film roles.

Ali Velshi was born in Kenya and raised in Toronto, to which his family immigrated when he was very small. Ali's father was the first Canadian of South Asian origin to be elected to the Legislative Assembly of Ontario. Ali is married to Philadelphia hedge fund manager Lori Wachs, and has two stepchildren. He commutes between Philadelphia and New York.

Christine Romans

Iowa native Christine Romans began her business reporting career in the Chicago commodities futures pits, which are still less hectic than life with her journalist husband Ed Tobin and their three young sons. By day, Christine is a business correspondent for CNN and host of *Your Bottom Line*.

When the financial system nearly collapsed in 2008, Christine brought nearly 15 years of economic and market reporting expertise to bear. Since then, she's hosted regular specials, including "Madoff: Secrets of a Scandal," "How the Wheels Came Off" (about the U.S. auto industry), and "In God We Trust" (about the relationship between faith and money).

Christine has won an Emmy for her work on globalization and the outsourcing of U.S. manufacturing and high-tech jobs, a MADD award for outstanding coverage of underage drinking issues, and National Foundation for Women Legislators award for coverage of money issues of importance to woman and government. She has also been honored twice by her alma mater, Iowa State University: as the 2006 Young Alumnus and in 2009 with the Schwartz Award for excellence in journalism.

She counts the last five years as the most productive of her life. She has covered a financial crisis, the worst recession since the Great

Depression, two hurricanes, a credit downgrade, a jobs crisis and political upheaval. She also had three baby boys and wrote her first book, drawing from her reporting from the financial crisis.

That book, *Smart is the New Rich: If You Can't Afford It—Put It Down,* was published in 2010. Unlike Ali, Christine does not hope this new book brings more film roles. She just wants to save enough for three college educations and retirement.

Index